IMMEDIATE SPEED

HOW TO SELL AND CLOSE TIMESHARE

David McEnery

DAVID MCENERY

Extreme appreciation to Mike Millisor, Rob Millisor and Mike Dudick, the owners of Breckenridge Grand Vacations.   Their vision created a company culture where, "We are the Best in Sales because we are the Best in Service."

Special thanks to David Stroeve for his integrity, leadership and friendship.

My gratitude to Glenn Brady for his insight.

Many accolades to Terri Cotter for her hard work in getting this book to print.

This book is for all of you who change people's lives each and every day.

Our Core Belief and Purpose

There is no "I" in "Team"! Our belief and purpose is to achieve SYNERGY: the interaction of two or more forces and energies so that their combined effect is greater than the sum of their individual efforts and effects.

Précis

David McEnery, a Registered Resort Professional (RRP), has been in the timeshare business since 1991. He demonstrates excellence in every aspect of his work. With personal net sales in 2010 of over $600k, reflecting a 41% closing rate, $4,911 VPG (Volume Per Guest) and 0% cancellation rate, his personal sales ability is unquestioned. Working at Grand Timber Lodge and Grand Lodge on Peak 7 since 2000, taking a couple tours a week, David has personally sold over $7.3 million net with a 25% close and a $3398 VPG. David personally assisted closing $10 million of the total sales volume achieved by the traditional sales line in 2010, and he has closed more than $80 million net on the traditional sales line. Our extremely successful sales team has generated in excess of $49 million in net sales for 2010, with a net closing rate of 18% and VPG of $3,638. But his real talent shines in the way he supports and motivates his team to create a synergy and to build a team that gets beyond natural competitive instincts, to work together for the benefit of the entire company. Our team focuses more on the life enhancement of travel provided by Vacation Ownership and less on the mechanics and lackluster logic of purchase (less boredom, more excitement and transference of energy).

At the core of the training developed by David is the "12 Steps to Success" Sales Formula. Each new broker completes a five-day intensive training in this highly detailed sales process, and the formula permeates ongoing training for all agents to ensure a consistent, informative and inspiring presentation for all tour guests. David trains the "12 Steps to Success" method in two parts – the *why* of the sales process and techniques and the *how* of the presentation steps – so that the agent will understand *why* each step in the sales process is necessary and *how* to apply these steps for success.

While the "12 Steps to Success" outline the information to be included in the presentation, David also developed a parallel technique, the "The Four Basics", to encourage engagement between tour guests and brokers, and sales management as "friends", and as "valued guests in our home."

David exudes a joy for living and for sharing the best of relationship; that essence permeates his sales team. Running through his entire professional and personal life is a single purpose: to be "in-spirit" and to inspire. The biggest compliment David's team receives is when a new owner says the company environment "has a wonderful energy", sometimes even asking if the company is hiring!

As described above, the "12 Steps to Success" and "Four Basics" programs have been developed to maximize sales, and have been successful in maximizing sales and VPG by incorporating a sense of cooperation and friendship among all parties involved in the sales presentation. The end result is a seamless process of welcoming the tour guest into the family, so that the final step involves acknowledgement of a new relationship rather than "closing the sale."

Intentions

The purpose of this book is for you to hone your skills and craft to a razor's edge. Use the margins in this book to take personal notes. When something moves you or when a brilliant idea happens upon you (an "aha" moment), write it down immediately. The purpose of this book is to summon up any hidden genius that lays dormant inside of you. It is meant to inspire you. Live, work and play in spirit. The Universe likes speed, thus the Universe loves <u>IMMEDIATE SPEED!</u>

To Sell: to deliver for money, goods, services or property. To attract prospective buyers, to be popular in the marketplace. To be approved of, to gain acceptance. To serve.

To Close: To join, unite, shut complete, to bring together all of the elements to end and finish. To surround and advance upon, so as to eliminate the possibility of escape. Not easily to acquire, scarce, as credit or money. Bound by mutual interest, loyalties or affections. The art of closing; conclusion, finish. Proximate in time, space and relationship, all encompassing.

"Preparation plus Perfect Action equals Success!"

~ McEneryism

"There really is only one great answer, one great solution for a problem. You must find that great answer, and apply it in each and every masterful presentation."

~ Yes

"Find out within the first 30 minutes what's important to them. The next 30 minutes, show them how to get it through timeshare. The last 30 minutes, have them show you how timeshare will help them realize their dreams, today."

~ 90 Minute Presentation

"If you want it done right, Master It!"

~ McEneryism

PART I

PERFORMANCE OF STRUCTURE

"It's what you learn after you *KNOW IT ALL* that counts."

~ John Wooden

Performance of Structure

Welcome to Performance of Structure. The world is changing quite rapidly, and only those who embrace change will succeed in the future. Is timeshare only good enough for 15 percent of the people who take a preview tour, or is it possible to close 30 or 40 percent of the people who come into a sales center? Since high quality vacations enhance the fundamental goals of most human beings by creating happier, healthier lives, it should not be inconceivable to close even 50 percent of those people with enough interest to at least have a look at vacation ownership.

With your past performance and these new goals in mind, it is imperative that fundamental change be implemented. Within the context of this training program, new techniques for delivering the story of timeshare will be presented, and invaluable new philosophies will be explained. Some of these new philosophies directly contradict traditional theories, but substantive change is the only reasonable way to accomplish what Jim Collins calls "Big Hairy Audacious Goals" in his book Good to Great.

Zig Ziglar gives sales seminars and motivational speeches all over the world on a regular basis. Since he has a new audience every time he gives a presentation, 90 percent of every speech contains the exact same material which he delivers with enthusiasm. He modifies 10 percent of every presentation to match the specific needs and interests of each respective audience. Using Zig Ziglar's approach to delivering exceptional speeches is the basis of this sales training. By developing a system to deliver well thought out, rehearsed, yet passionate presentations to each and every client with customized messages tailored to the specific needs of your clients, it will be possible to achieve sales results unparalleled in the annals of timeshare.

Both Lawrence Olivier and Yule Brynner gave each performance as if it were opening night because they believed that the people seeing the performances were seeing them for the first time. They earnestly wanted to deliver their performances with every ounce of enthusiasm and passion they possibly could. They didn't just go through the motions of a script. They wanted to give a perfect performance each and every time they got on stage. As a result, they earned a standing ovation at the conclusion of every show. That is the essence of structure in the delivery of a sales presentation. The goal is to make sure that the sales presentation touches the life of every client regardless of whether or not they make a purchase. The value of every sales presentation is found in providing motivation for people to realize the value of personal relationships with family and friends. If sales representatives help enough people improve their lives, they will gain improvement in their own lives both financially and otherwise.

The traditional theories associated with selling timeshare have always emphasized the importance of doing a thorough client profile, and obtaining a vacation commitment from your client. Without these two components, most sales training programs suggest that a sale cannot be accomplished. However, if you have an intrinsic understanding that all human beings are motivated by essentially the same core needs, then the value of attempting to identify and understand every individual becomes significantly less important. In other words, an extensive client profile will not be necessary in order to achieve a very high level of sales success. However, every presentation needs to be so passionate and persuasive that it brings change to the way clients perceive their relationships, and how they strive to achieve the most important things in their lives. This philosophy is about changing people's lives rather than just selling timeshare. You must use your intuitive skills to impact people's lives in a positive way and success will follow.

"Progressive improvements by doing everything that little bit better, thus aiming for even higher standards."

~ Kaizen

"Intuition is the ability to see the unseen."

~ McEneryism

Chapter 1

GO FROM MEDIOCRE TO MIRACULOUS!

"When you're green you *GROW*."

Go from Mediocre to Miraculous!

To understand who you are is to know that you are destined for greatness. What you believe and conceive, you will achieve. You have a higher self, and what you ask of yourself, you will be granted. Your requests and choices come from your own sense of personal potency, and your caring about others. When you make those choices from the center of your higher self, they are best for you and for the others in your life. Your own optimism will become everyone's best energy. Thus, if you are a true sales professional, you are always in a position to be at your professional best.

To be in this position means that you see yourself positively, and as a valued resource. You maintain a high degree of mental readiness, snapping back quickly from rejection. You are becoming positive, prepared, reliable, focused, caring, serious, better, different, resourceful and professional while maintaining directed energy. Most of all, you are fun and joyful, thereby increasing sales and increasing profits. You have created a conscious process in which your attitude, behavior and actions create a standard of excellence. You are proactive, and make things happen rather than waiting, and reacting. You are a risk-taking, creative, focused and decisive selling machine. "No" means "Not Yet," and "Yes" means "Trial Close," and when your intuition tells you that your client is ready, "Close the Deal." When you listen to your intuition it connects you to a greater knowledge. You are synergistic, and you project a win/win relationship in all of your selling and closing endeavors. Because of this, you have earned the right to all of your dreams, self actualization and autonomy.

"Do you have joy in your life? Do you give joy to others?"

~ Bodhi

Attributes for Success

You have been chosen for success. You are the greatest of all time!

You must be outstanding. You must be extraordinary. You must be committed. You must be persistent. You must be flexible enough to change. You must always take action. Thus, you will be a successful salesperson.

Impact and improve your communication. Words are important. Tonality must be varied, and physiology (body language) is key. Your sales presentation should be centered, and based upon on trust, solutions and urgency.

Peak performance is a result of being in a peak state of mind where attitude is everything. A state of passion creates peak performance. Harness the power of passion. Turn your passion and conviction into belief, and change your state of mind into a positive mental attitude that becomes habit not only for you, but for your colleagues and clients. You must change, and state outwardly to the universe that you are making the changes necessary to become the world's best timeshare salesperson! The secret to becoming a successful timeshare salesperson is that you must live your life in joy and gratitude. When you possess joy and gratitude in your daily life, these gifts will encompass all areas of your life, and transcend into your business life.

Become the best by establishing rapport quickly through a feeling of commonality. People like people like themselves. People do not care how much you know until they know how much you care. You cannot tell anyone what they will get. Give your clients the experience of your passion, conviction and feelings of owning and using timeshare.

The number one secret in selling is that people are fearful of, and do not like change. Your only job is to get them to trust you enough to focus on all of the benefits, showing them it's better than the alternative (that it is okay to change). Fear will turn into pleasure, and pleasure is what your clients will receive. Create a compelling future, have your clients step into their future, and describe how they will feel using the vacation products and services you have to offer.

<u>Chapter 2</u>

<u>THE PARADIGM SHIFT</u>

"Yesterday was the past. Today is the *PRESENT*."

The Paradigm Shift

Do not Prejudge

If your clients are nervous about the sales presentation and only express interest in their gift, and want to leave as soon as possible, what responses would they likely give? What information would they put on a survey? How would they answer your questions?

If you must prejudge, be sure to prejudge in a positive way. Find something you like or love about your clients and make friends with them!

As a sales professional in the vacation ownership industry, you must realize that it is always you and two other people. Most of the time your clients will not change. But, some will change, and therein lies the reward. Changing your clients' lives for the better is incredibly exciting and fulfilling. You must change your ways to survive and thrive. What are you doing to get better? What are you willing to give up to get better? Are you changing? In the vacation ownership business, it truly is the survival of the fittest!

The Little Train that Could

Liam Meirow is the 15 year old son of one of our brokers, Drew Meirow, whom I have the pleasure of seeing grow into a fine young man. In August, 2011, Liam won a grueling obstacle course race in Colorado that is a based on speed and athletic ability. He competed with seven thousand entrants and finished first. Did he win because of his belief that he could? Did he win because of his enthusiasm? Did he win because he didn't know any better? The challenges and course changes were paramount and this illustrates the enlightening power of preparation and the gift of being *new*!

Change is in an instant. Embrace oncoming change!
The light at the end of the tunnel is not an oncoming train.
The light you see is prosperity, success and pure joy!

Chapter 3

<u>WORKING IN SALES</u>

"LIVE every day of your life!"

Working in Sales

Confucius says: "If you love what you do, you will never work a day in your life."

You must love working in sales and love selling vacation ownership. There are two stories that come to mind regarding a new hire and a seasoned salesperson that we will call "Be Quicker of Mind than of Tongue." The first story is about a new broker who came to work for us with much hope and enthusiasm. He studied hard, was making headway and becoming successful. Unfortunately, he was unable to maintain this success because he was holding onto resentments. The moment that he said outwardly how he truly felt was the end of his six month career. Simply stated, he said, "I *hate* all of these clients." He realized that his heart was not in the timeshare business, and he left the company.

The second story is about a seasoned broker who would pick up his survey sheet, and then study it for a minimum of ten minutes while his clients were sitting in the lobby. He would grimace and prejudge his clients, finding all the reasons that he thought they wouldn't be able to buy. After making this poor assessment, he would complain to other brokers that his clients were broke or any other mean and derogatory phrases he could imagine. This would create negative energy within an otherwise upbeat environment. We addressed this inappropriate behavior and this broker took personal responsibility and with a positive plan of action, corrected his attitude. Within two weeks of his living in gratitude, treating his clients with kindness and always finding "something he liked about them," he became a superstar again. The point is that *your perception is your reality*.

The way to become a top sales professional is not through revelation; it is by persistent hard work. The old expressions, "Salespeople are born, not made," or "He's a born salesman," are not true. Like any great athlete, the more thought and hard work you put into your craft, the better you become. You must continuously learn, adjust, change and discover new ways to grow. Listen only to the top performers in your field or in your company. Ask them questions and bounce your ideas off them. The greatest compliment you can pay someone is to try to be more like them. Associate yourself with the winners and avoid the complainers and the blamers. Most importantly, don't ever become a complainer or a blamer.

You can aspire to be the best, but will you ever really be the best you can be? Won't there always be some room for improvement? Know that you can always improve, and that as the world changes, so too must you adjust your presentation. Take notes that you can review, and incorporate different techniques into your presentations. Always try new ideas, and discard the old ones that do not work. Sales is a very dynamic career field. It moves with the beliefs of the community. What worked in the 1950's doesn't work anymore! Society is much more savvy, sophisticated and educated. Remember, when you're green you grow, and when you're ripe, you rot! If you want to be a top producer, you must continuously challenge your comfort zone and break through your personal barriers. You must take action and implement what you have learned. You must take your thoughts to a process.

Selling is an inside job. You must be a great person to have a great sales career. Anyone without integrity and joy in their life will not last long as a salesperson. Your clients are looking for more than a product, they are looking for solutions to their problems. Their favorite radio station is WIIFM – What's In It For Me! They want solutions that will satisfy their wants and fill their needs, and more importantly, they desire someone they can rely on and trust. They are buying you more than they are buying your product because when you get right down to it, your product is not much different from that of your competition. You are different, and you are better. You must help your clients!

A career in sales is the hardest job you'll ever love. You will face continual rejection which you must let slide right off you as if you were made of Teflon. You have unique difficulties and challenges every day which most people never encounter. Build your resilience and keep your optimism. Know that this is all part of your job. On the other hand, you also have the unique privilege of controlling your income, and you enjoy more freedoms than most others have in their jobs. If you have a tough enough personality, and if you keep the right perspective and attitude, a career in sales is unmatched in terms of personal satisfaction. To have a successful, long-lasting sales career, you must always live in gratitude, and become a constantly happy and joyous individual.

Your power is to design the life you want by giving your clients the lives they want. Your energy, power and enthusiasm will make you rich, not just financially, but rich in abundance in every aspect of your life. If you have been having challenges in the past, it has no effect on the greatness that you can have in your future. All that matters is what you do right now. Once you have the desire and commitment to become excellent, your dreams will become part of your daily reality. Remember, expand your comfort zone and conquer your fears. Become a master of understanding human behavior. Ask yourself the following questions aloud and answer them aloud. This is the first step to becoming a Master Closer. Your journey throughout your sales career will always begin with the first step.

What makes people do what they do?

Why do people take action steps every day?

Why are small, simple changes very important?

Why must I be focused to get what I want?

Why do I focus on things that I want most?

Why should I demand more from myself?

Am I living in inspiration (in spirit)?

Do my actions show my desperation?

Am I okay when I am dissatisfied because I know things will get better?

How will I master my financial success?

Why should I study successful people?

Why should I study the Master Closers?

Why should I immerse myself in the sales process?

Why should I practice off the field?

Why should I come to play every day?

Am I taking a walk in the woods, or am I coming to hunt?

Am I jaded?

Is this moment new, fresh and alive?

Am I using all of my brain power to get the best results?

What changes do I have to make in my life to be the best that I can be?

Do I want the power and the ability to live fearlessly?

Am I successful?

Do I already know my outcome?

Am I clear on my goals?

Do I always take an action step?

Do I believe in myself, and do I believe I can achieve and receive anything I desire?

Ask yourself all of these questions, and go through them again and again and make sure that you have progression and positive responses to all of them.

The difference between selling and closing is a credit card. Great closers are great storytellers. Effective salespeople must excite and engage their clients. To gain pleasure and profit, you as a salesperson must tell all of your stories in color. Use great diction, and consider all of the senses. A salesperson is simply a business actor – so are all great leaders. You must spend hours rehearsing to give the performance of a lifetime, every time.

In a two hour timeframe, a timeshare salesperson must energize and excite a potential owner about a better way to vacation, and show why spending an average of $20,000 today makes more financial sense than paying rent to hotels for the next 20 years. Typically, the prospects who come in for a tour do not intend to buy anything. They are just willing to give up a couple hours of their vacation time listening to a "sales pitch" in exchange for discount lodging, show tickets, or some other marketing gift. Many times a couple has entered a pact warning each other not to show any interest during the presentation. Also typical in the timeshare industry, the sales presentation ends with a "Yes" or "No" answer. There is no "Maybe" – a client walking away without an ownership interest never returns to buy later.

Some people will attend several presentations before finally buying a timeshare, and it is not only because of the program features and benefits that they decide to buy, but the personality and the skills of the salesperson they speak with that causes them to take an action step. There are basic steps in core areas that must be followed in each presentation, but these steps are encased in your own personality and energy. They are surrounded by your integrity, your sense of humor and your unique style.

This book is intended to get your game on track. Your inner game is in your head and in your heart. Your outer game is your methods and techniques. The law of cause and effect has everything to do with salesmanship. Everything happens for a reason. Your thoughts are the causes for your circumstances and success in your life. You become what you think all the time. So think about what you want and how you are going to get it. Think like a top salesperson who always has a plan to stay a top performer. Decide on what you want to earn, be grateful for the ability to accomplish that objective, and go earn it. With this optimism and high expectation of yourself and your clients, success will follow. This is mind over matter! As you become mentally fit, your self esteem and self confidence will go through the roof. Your actions will become ambitious, courageous, and persistent. You will continue to become the best you can by overcoming any obstacles that stand in your way. The most important thing to remember is "for every action there is a reaction." Simply applied, your actions will be positive, and the universe's reactions will be desirable.

Eight Actions of Selling

1. Get motivated.

2. Identify your weaknesses, and turn them into strengths.

3. Surround yourself with positive people.

4. Take pride in your physical, mental, emotional and spiritual health.

5. Practice positive reinforcement (I believe in me).

6. Visualize yourself selling and closing, welcoming your newest owners.

7. Visualize yourself as the Number One Salesperson.

8. Take directed and purposeful actions toward your goals on a daily basis.

Becoming a professional timeshare salesperson does not happen overnight. Mastering the techniques and philosophies within this book will take time, discipline and practice. You will only get out of this business what you are willing to put into it. Most successful sales professionals continue growing and learning as the sales environment evolves and changes. If you wanted to become a professional athlete, what must you do? If you had the desire to become a doctor or lawyer, what must you do? The answer to both questions will lead you to great success selling timeshare if you continually study and practice.

Successful salespeople have similar qualities. They exhibit a tremendous work ethic, they learn from their mistakes and they continue growing by reading sales books, listening to CDs and attending training seminars. Invest in yourself. Money is an energy and you must make yourself better. Spread the wealth. Go out into the marketplace and purchase items that you believe will help you get better.

The most successful salespeople only associate and role play with the best of their colleagues, and they know their product. They internalize true conviction with regard to what the product can and cannot do for their clients. Success leaves clues, and successful salespeople remain committed on a continuous basis to understanding the behavior that leads to greatness.

The Vacation Ownership product is sold with passion and conviction. Most importantly, it is an emotional sale.

Beautifully Stated

"As we grow up, we learn that even the one person that wasn't supposed to ever let you down probably will. You will have your heart broken probably more than once and it's harder every time. You'll break hearts too, so remember how it felt when yours was broken. You'll fight with your best friend. You'll blame a new love for things an old one did. You'll cry because time is passing too fast, and you'll eventually lose someone you love. So take too many pictures, laugh too much, and love like you've never been hurt because every sixty seconds you spend upset is a minute of happiness you'll never get back. Don't be afraid that your life will end, be afraid that it will never begin."

~ Anonymous

Where could you apply Beautifully Stated?

When would you make use of this passage?

What did you get from this story?

How did this make you feel?

Why do you feel this wisdom is important?

Chapter 4

THE PRESENTATION

"Great actors *EARN* more than teachers."

The Presentation

When selling becomes a procedure, closing sales ceases to be a problem. If selling is not a procedure, success in sales will always be a problem. Designing and implementing a prescribed formula for success is the foundation of a great sales presentation. Systems yield structure, and structure is the foundation for success. Even with a powerful presentation, it is not possible to inspire every single client to purchase. No product or service in existence can be sold to 100 percent of the public on a consistent basis. However, success in sales can be maximized by making sure that every sales presentation follows a specific prescription targeting a specific demographic group. The individual presentations can be modified slightly according to the special circumstances of different clients, but the structure inherent to the system will greatly improve the likelihood of creating a positive impact. Of course, every sales presentation – especially structured presentations - must also be delivered with a great deal of spontaneity and enthusiasm in order to achieve the desired results.

Vacation Ownership is not a sought-after good; thank goodness it isn't or we all would have a decrease in pay. Think about that for a while! If everyone could do our job of closing a sale for $20,000 or more in 90 minutes, we definitely would earn far less. Imagine if everyone just walked in and said "I'm here to buy" and they really did. This would cause a serious lack of unique timeshare sales individuals and we would be just like everyone else (sometimes known as order-takers). Since your clients come in without any desire, and sometimes without any knowledge of the product, your presentation must be focused, concise and customized to your client. You must be entertaining, informative and persuasive.

The art of delivery is very simple. It's not what you say, but how you say it. Understanding how to deliver the information and concepts inherent to the sales process is the key to creating a persuasive and powerful presentation. The only way to make a sale is to speak with someone. Without a client to talk with, it is impossible to make a sale. The only bad client is no client. Remember, live in gratitude, and attempt to remove all negative slang that degrades your clients or your profession in any way. Remove prejudices from your thoughts because your thoughts eventually become your actions. Use kind words regarding your clients, your fellow salespeople and the industry. Really, it is all up to you to be a consummate professional. Be kind. You really never know who is listening…including you. This is one of the most important things to remember in this business, and why it is imperative to deliver a full and complete presentation to every client. This is also one of the most difficult philosophies to internalize. It takes discipline. It is natural behavior to prejudge, to measure up your client and then make a determination as to whether or not they will be worth the effort. However, prejudging clients invariably costs lots of money in the long run because many buyers will be missed, and significant commissions lost.

If you have a profound message or a great story to share with clients that will impact the way they view their own values, then share that message or story with every client regardless of their demographic grouping. The objective is to provide information that will offer solutions to problems associated with past experiences, and give hope that the future can be different. Do not change the message or story with every presentation. Since the message or story delivers a broad based concept, keep the structure of every presentation consistent regardless of the audience.

The system for selling timeshare involves the categorization of clients into two separate and distinct groups – Owners of Timeshare and Non-Owners of Timeshare. Most of every presentation will be the same regardless of client grouping. However, the rest will be tailored in one of two directions depending upon whether or not your clients already own timeshare. Understanding verbal and non-verbal styles of communication such as reading body language and knowing which of your clients is the decision maker remain very important. However, it will be easy to master the techniques associated with delivering a powerful presentation if the presentation is structured and consistent with only subtle variations based upon the ownership orientation of your clients.

In the simplest of terms, there exist only two types of people who will ever take a timeshare presentation – Owners of Timeshare and Non-Owners of Timeshare. Every presentation must deliver a broad based message with value to both groups. However, timeshare owners will purchase for reasons quite different from those who do not already own timeshare. Non-Owners of Timeshare purchase in order to have the hope that they will be able to accomplish their future vacation dreams and aspirations by having a more consistent vacation plan. They purchase timeshare in order to increase the quality of their vacation accommodations, and to have the opportunity to stay in safer environments. They also purchase in order to achieve stronger financial stability. These are all very compelling reasons for everyone to own timeshare. However, Timeshare Owners have already taken the leap of faith necessary to believe that their lives will be better with a timeshare ownership interest.

Timeshare Owners must be reminded why they initially purchased, but they will acquire additional time for very different reasons. For Timeshare Owners, adding weeks to their portfolio will create deeper and closer connections with the people they love, and provide a mechanism for them to enjoy healthier and happier lives. The additional investment will make them more financially secure as well. As people progress in their careers and get closer to retirement, they will generally have more free time available. How they choose to spend that time is vitally important to their personal happiness and well being.

Buying the first week of timeshare is the start of securing a lifetime of stability, quality and happiness. Timeshare owners must acquire additional time to properly round out their portfolio for retirement. When people start planning for retirement by establishing a 401K plan, should their initial investment also be their last? Planning for retirement is not an event. It is a process. If a person's first contribution to their retirement plan became their last such investment, how financially secure would they be in their retirement years? If people have the discipline to make regular contributions to their emotional well being and financial security on an annual basis through timeshare ownership, they will live happier and more productive lives. Continuing to invest in what's important – the people and relationships in life – will in fact improve the quality of life for everyone. At the end of the day, aren't the quality of personal relationships and the lives touched over a lifetime the most valuable things in life?

Timeshare owners also have a desire to complement and improve the quality of their ownership experiences. Additional ownership provides more options, and more opportunity to enjoy quality time with the people most important to them. Oftentimes people will buy something small to get started, planning to upgrade to more time or more space in the future.

"Improving your sales techniques is like fine tuning a Ferrari. You must turn the screwdriver *just a little* or risk losing the race."

~ McEneryism

"You are either resisting or accepting constructive coaching. You must choose when you will live in acceptance, otherwise you will die in resistance."

~ Coach

"When the student is ready, the master will appear."

~ Confucius

Chapter 5

<u>ATTITUDE</u>

"BELIEVE you can and you will."

Attitude

Believe it, Conceive it, and Achieve it!

In selling, attitude is everything. Selling is the transference of energy. Have you ever been around someone who just brought you down? For some reason, you felt they were sucking the energy right out of you, and you had to get away from them. On the other hand, have you ever met someone so upbeat and positive that you didn't want them to leave? They were empowering! In person to person selling, your attitude alone can sell the product - completely by itself.

Several years ago, a company hired a few people who had never previously sold timeshare. Normally, only those individuals with an extensive sales background or timeshare experience would ever be considered. Through this process, the company hired a woman named Joy. Joy had never sold timeshare, and had very little sales experience of any kind. She worked in the restaurant business prior to being hired. Grateful for being given a chance to sell timeshare, Joy lit up like a Christmas tree.

Back then, the company did not have a core training program. New hires were just handed reading materials to study. Joy became our top agent in her first month. She sold more than $300,000 that first month, making more than $32,000. However, when management went to help complete her transactions, Joy's clients generally had no working knowledge or understanding of the product they were purchasing. They were really buying Joy's enthusiasm. She was so excited and energetic on every tour her clients believed that the company she represented constituted the best thing since sliced bread. They just wanted what she was selling. Her clients were thinking to themselves, "If someone is this excited about the product, it must be good. We've got to have some of it."

A few months later, Joy started learning how the product functions, and more specifically, how the trading works. She discovered some of the perceived faults (perception is reality) of timeshare. The newness of the job wore off, and the work environment and office politics became important to her. Nothing is ever perfect, and after a while, everyone starts noticing how green the grass appears to be across the street. Within a short time from her euphoric beginning, Joy's sales pace started to change. Her sales performance levels dropped, and continued to drop as she learned and became comfortable with her surroundings. Her career in this business only lasted four months, but she made more in one month than she had ever previously made in a whole year. Always remember "Joy!"

Attitude is everything in selling timeshare, and maintaining a positive, enthusiastic attitude will make you extremely successful. Having said this, doing it is much more difficult than simply writing it down on paper. We all are human. We have social lives that can affect our performance, and we do go through sales slumps from time to time. It is also very easy to become frustrated with the internal workings of the company, its policies and politics. However, none of this matters because you have chosen a profession where your attitude can single handedly make or destroy your performance. So how does one keep the enthusiasm?

There are four focuses one must understand to keep a healthy positive attitude. These are not the only ones, but in the timeshare business, they are core ingredients to success. Take the time to consciously practice the appropriate behavior and discipline so that when you walk up and say "Hello" to your next customer, you have what it takes to make the sale.

"Attitude is Altitude!"

~ Breckenridge

Exclusively Associate With Positive People

When you come to work, you should only have one purpose - to help clients change their lives for the better by making a sale. Do not hang around people who are negative. Do not sit and listen to fellow agents complain or explain why their clients didn't purchase. Stay away from people complaining about things because their negativity can be contagious. In most cases, these people are not top performers. They are rather mediocre sales agents with a short career in this business. You need to save your energy for your clients. If you expend your energy on non-essential conversation, you won't have what is needed when it counts.

Wipe Your Feet at the Door

Wiping your feet at the door is not easy, but it is essential. Turn off the outside world because none of your problems are going to matter to your clients anyway. In selling timeshare, it's all about them, not you. Take a few minutes before every tour to mentally prepare. Envision doing a great presentation, and getting a "Yes." Some sales representatives stay physically active in order to summon up or release energy, so that when they come to work, it's all about their client. Your activities, whether negative or positive, outside of the office, affect your business inside the office. Find your own *positive* solution.

Nothing is Perfect

One fundamental truth is the fact that everything will change because nothing is perfect. In life, when things are not perfect nature will make adjustments. Those natural adjustments could mean survival or extinction because mother nature has no emotion. Therefore you must be willing to live in this state of acceptance and gratitude with as much enthusiasm, passion and conviction that you can muster on a daily basis. You must believe, conceive and achieve it in your own state of being that truly not everything in your life or other's lives is perfect. You've heard that the only guarantees in life are death and taxes. Well, another one could be added, and that one is change. There must be room for acceptance because a perfectionist drives everyone crazy. The mechanisms of this product, the members of the team, the culture of the company and the operations of the resort will always be changing. As these things change, you must change with them in order to remain successful. You can choose to view any situation as if the glass is half full rather than half empty. The art of accepting change is to use it to your own advantage because any resistance to change will definitely be your extinction. Nothing is perfect.

Responsibility

The easy way out of any negative situation is to blame problems on anyone or anything other than ones' self. However, this type of thinking does nothing positive. In fact, it teaches acceptance of having absolutely no control over your life. A career in selling will always have its ups and downs. If you take a look at the week, month or year, some will always be better than others. When on a roll, tape yourself or meticulously think through what you are doing and keep repeating it. When you go through many clients without a sale, accept it and forgive yourself. Why let a short period of time affect your attitude and self confidence? It is a guarantee that everyone will have a down week or month. Like water running down the back of a duck, sales professionals who forget about sales slumps are the ones who will succeed. Too often, when sales slumps occur, normal reactions and thought patterns tend to be negative - "The tours were bad", "It's the management's fault," or "The resort has issues," etc. When this happens, look within and take personal inventory of your attitude. What have you done to stay current and grow? What actions have you taken to help position your attitude and remain positive?

When you accept personal responsibility, you take control of your life. A little known secret is that when you're in a slump, the reason why the slump began is that you needed it. This sounds strange, but somebody somewhere is attempting to teach you a lesson. Your lesson might be humility. Your lesson might be gratitude. Your lesson might be about your ego. A great coach, a mentor, once mentioned that you must keep your ego in check. As a matter of fact, he described EGO as Edging God Out, whereas truly great human beings always live in gratitude. Your lesson might be the sales slump itself. The reason for a slump is that you are trying to sell people just like yourself. You are taking the path of least resistance and are attempting to sell the people you like. Remember, we always like people like ourselves - we like people just like us. The challenge is to find something you like about all of your clients, and everyone you meet. A Master Closer once gave the best advice ever. She said, "Find something you love about your clients. Anyone can love the lovable, but it takes a master to love the unlovable." When you are in a slump, you are going inward and feeling sorry for yourself, and as a result becoming selfish. You must have the courage to go outward and live in gratitude regarding your livelihood. A slump is only temporary. Selling and closing is not a sprint, it's a marathon!

Because of the fact that the profession of selling inherently has its ups and downs, it is important to realize that it is what you do and learn when you are down that will truly make you successful. The purpose of life is to gain wisdom and courage as these phrases emphasize;

"God, grant me the serenity to accept the things I cannot change, the courage to change the things I can, and the wisdom to know the difference."

~ Reinhold Niebuhr

"Under the bold guidance of the spirit
wander into the studio of the master
and after a time he shall say,
'I have nothing more to teach you.'
And now you have become a master."

~ James Allen

"Self control is strength;
right thought is mastery;
calmness is power."

~ James Allen

"There are three kinds of business:
My Business. None of My Business. God's Business."

~ Higher Power

Chapter 6

CLIENT BODY LANGUAGE

"Study the *SCIENCE* of body language because a body never lies."

Client Body Language

Body Language Says It All

You must meet and greet your newest owners with great body language – a warm smile and open arms while leaning your heart toward your clients' hearts. You can establish genuine bonding with your clients simply by looking them directly in the eye – looking closely enough to determine their eye color. Eyes serve as the window and mirror of the soul.

You should display a welcoming attitude, and envision your clients as your newest owners. You should also use their first names early and often. People enjoy hearing their own names, and using their names will help establish the fact that you are kind, caring and trustworthy. Clients do not care how much you know until they know how much you care about them and their needs. Therefore, it is important that your body language communicates a "Welcome to our home" attitude so that your clients feel at home even before you start assessing their body language.

You must remember that your clients are really two separate and distinct individuals doing business as one. In order to consummate a sale, the body language from all parties must be positive and congruent. Yule Brynner received more contiguous standing ovations than any other stage performer. His response to this fact is essential. He said "Every audience has seen my performance only once. Therefore, I give it my all every time." Body language represents the choreography of a stage play in the sales presentation. The objective is to earn a standing ovation from clients in the form of trust and new business.

You should start the sales process by making an assessment as to which of your clients is more animated displaying open body language, better eye contact and an open stance. Nodding in a positive manner, or moving closer to the sales materials when presented also indicate interest. Your big challenge is to avoid ignoring, but rather focus upon the less enthusiastic client. You should then use the more open client to help engage the more challenging client in conversation.

Always bear in mind that your clients are two unique individuals acting as one on their way to saying yes to the offer of ownership as a team.

The body language clients use to convey that they will become new owners is wonderful and exciting to observe. Master Closers take notice of "The Look" – when their clients stop and look at one another silently in a kind and loving way saying to each other without words that, "It's okay with me. If you want it, we'll buy it." This single one second gesture is a sure sign of a sale when both parties are leaning in, smiling and expressive. The "What's in it for me?" questions have been answered, and the sale is a done deal even before your clients verbally agree to become owners.

There is wisdom in the saying "Laughter is the best medicine." When your clients are laughing and having fun, they feel the emotion and love life. When they display cues such as smiles, hand holding and a reconnection of their love, the observant sales professional knows the sale has been achieved even before his clients realize it. At this time, Master Closers take the opportunity to compliment their clients, and let them know that it is okay for them to purchase today. Master closers remain calm, positive and encouraging. Master closers have "kind eyes" that help them achieve win/win results. Sales professionals who transfer positive, upbeat energy to their clients will succeed in making nine out of ten clients want the product, and those sales professionals who continue to sell, no matter what, will get the majority of their clients to have the courage to "Just do it today."

Body language is the choreography of a stage play in every sales presentation. The objective is to earn standing ovations from clients in the form of trust and new business. Watch for cues and clues, and know when the sale is made. Transfer positive, upbeat energy to your clients and give them the courage to take an action step.

Understanding client body language is a very important part of the sales process. Sometimes, if the product is right for your clients, all you have to do is make them comfortable, and the sale is fairly easy to close. Simply smiling as you are talking to your client, standing without your arms crossed in a non-confrontational way, and acknowledging that you understand your clients and care about their needs can often make a sale because this relaxes your clients. Master closers have "kind eyes" that help demonstrate kindness, care, and sincerity.

Look in the mirror at home before leaving for work, and pretend that you are speaking to your newest owner. Envision your clients and practice kindness and gratitude so that your entire being displays "kind eyes" even before you meet your morning clients. Now, you have envisioned the sale, and you have prepared yourself to be inspired which truly means in-spirit. Preparation plus perfect action equals success!

You want to take your clients to a "happy place" in their minds – a good time filled with fun and exciting vacation memories. When this happens, negative body language such as no eye contact, folded arms, and clients glancing at their watches goes away. Clients who are feeling positive do not fold or stack papers or ask for a business card when the presentation is still in progress. Bringing clients to that "happy place" represents your opportunity to earn standing ovations and win/win results for everyone.

Ignoring a client's body language can often prevent a sale because your client may not be agreeing with you or they may feel uncomfortable. Asking a buying question or trying to close your clients when their body language is showing that they are nervous, confused or unhappy can often lead to a lost sale. Many times fear, worry or confusion stand in the way of your clients wanting to buy.

Early in the sales presentation, your clients are usually anxious and confused, and as a result, they are often standing with their arms folded and avoiding eye contact. They may appear fidgety or nervous. That's perfectly understandable and expected. After all, wouldn't you be the same way if you were about to meet someone who has a reputation for trying to high pressure people into buying something? This is why it's important in the beginning of the sales process to relax and earn the trust of your clients by showing them you care about their needs. You can even say that your product may not be for them. Trying to sell your clients before you understand their vacation needs will only make your clients more apprehensive.

Once the presentation starts, if your clients are becoming more involved and moving closer to a purchase, the wife will usually put her purse down and they will both start leaning over the desk and begin exploring some of the information you are explaining, such as the exchange options. You want to get your clients as involved as much as possible. Have them look through a trade book or ask them simple, involving questions. Asking your clients to do something with their hands will often start the process of opening their arms and minds to vacation ownership. Having them pick up something, or show you some of their family photos are easy ways to shift their body language. A client with his arms folded behind his head and leaning back in the chair is sometimes a sign of relaxation and open mindedness. It can also mean your client is so relaxed that he is not taking you seriously. If your clients are not taking you seriously, make sure you get them involved in your presentation as quickly as possible.

Always get your clients some water – the human body always needs cold, refreshing water. As simple as it sounds, getting your clients water shows you care about them. This simple gesture will often get them to become more relaxed. Sometimes your clients will tell you they understand when they really don't. A furrowed brow, no eye contact or slight frown will often tell you if your clients are either not agreeing or are confused. It's very important to ask your clients qualifying questions to ensure that they really do understand and agree with what you are saying. Direct eye contact, a relaxed brow and "smiling eyes" all show that your clients are agreeable and usually understand you. With combative or suspicious customers, it's important to always remain calm, positive and encouraging. Never reduce yourself to arguing with them. Remember, you can't sell everyone, and you shouldn't waste your positive energy on an evil-spirited person. As a sales professional, you never, ever have to take abuse. Your goal is to always have your clients leave happy regardless of the outcome.

The sales presentation is your domain, and you are always in control! Talented salespeople always know that they're in control. Master Closers let their clients feel that they are in control by leading them in a direction that flows to a positive end result. The word "control" means that you are always proceeding in a precise manner, moving ahead with purpose. Even a Master Closer, at times, loses control. However they recognize it and immediately do something different to resolve the situation.

Master Closers will take a break during the presentation and give their clients a task such as creating a vacation dream list from the resort directory. The Master Closer will then go outside to get some fresh air. This activity will elicit some fresh thoughts to summon direction back into the presentation. Your purpose is to change your own emotional state because Energy Plus Motion equals Emotion. At this time you will be getting a message from your higher self, or higher power that will be beneficial to all concerned.

Changing your own emotional state allows you to change the emotional state of your clients because you will be transferring positive energy, thereby regaining control. This method dissipates tension by removing one of you from an uncomfortable situation. This movement will change a negative into a more favorable circumstance. When you return, it will be a fun and fresh start. You successfully removed the feeling that you could "cut the tension with a knife," and you will be able to resume selling and closing.

As you show your property, those who are about to buy will often begin holding hands, or ask permission to smoke. Both are usually great signs of interest. It's best to let them have a smoke if it's appropriate for your facility. If your resort has a great view, put your clients in the picture and let them sit in the places that will let them relax and experience your facility as it should be enjoyed. It's important not to bother your clients while they are taking it all in. Don't throw a stone into your clients' pool of water.

At the closing table, your clients will sometimes be nervous and will show it by the wife putting her purse on her lap and holding it shut. That is not a good sign. One tactic is to ask your clients a question unrelated to timeshare that will take them back to a "happy place."

"A person's body language cannot lie. You are a human lie detector, seeing what is not said. You must have the courage and wisdom to ask tough questions which will lead to a sale."

~ Skinny Branches

"Are you willing to do the research to become the best? Do you have an achievable goal to reach your highest potential? Are you willing to do the hard work to become the Greatest Of All Time? "

~ G.O.A.T.

1. What periodicals, articles, blogs, online information, editorials, commentaries, news pieces, expose's and any other research regarding body language can you find to study?

2. What book on body language are you willing to purchase immediately?

3. Why is studying and mastering the art of understanding body language vitally important in your timeshare sales career? Why must you master this craft in order to become your very best?

_____

_____

_____

_____

_____

_____

_____

"We enjoy the journey and we love earning standing ovations.
It is our moment to shine."

~ McEneryism

Chapter 7

THE FIVE CORE MOTIVATIONAL NEEDS

"WIIFM … What's In It For Me?"

The Five Core Motivational Needs

According to Abraham Maslow, human beings have a hierarchy of needs. The most basic physical needs include air, water, food, and shelter. Once these needs have been fulfilled, humans look for security and stability. Then social needs such as love, acceptance and a sense of belonging become important. Finally, humans seek out self actualization - the need for fulfillment, the need to become all that one is capable of becoming.

In this day and age, most people in the western world have achieved the very basic or fundamental needs. However, everyone experiences a life long struggle to achieve and maintain their desired level for security, love, acceptance and self actualization. Since life is significantly more complex today than it was a few hundred years ago, the Five Core Motivational Needs we will focus on here include:

Health

Safety, Security

Love, Sense of Belonging, Acceptance

Growth, Financial Security

Better Quality of Life

Linking the benefits of timeshare ownership with these Five Core Motivational Needs will result in a significant increase in sales success because everyone, no matter what their station in life may be, wants these same things. Everyone wants happiness, health, peace of mind, financial security and close friendships. Everyone wants to have the hope that the future will be better than the past. Everyone wants to become the person they were meant to be. Everyone wants to be accepted, and truly loved. Everyone wants to be respected, and everyone wants to feel that their life has made a difference. Everyone wants to believe that they have done the right thing for themselves, their families and their society.

Everyone wants to live the life they feel they are capable of living. Everyone wants to feel a certain level of internal satisfaction. Human beings' highest purpose is to achieve autonomy and self-actualization.

If taking regular timeshare vacations enhances health and longevity, who would say no? If timeshare ownership increases the sense of safety and security, who would say no? If timeshare ownership brings love, acceptance and a sense of belonging, who would say no? If timeshare ownership enhances growth and financial security, who would say no? If timeshare ownership yields a better overall quality of life, who would say no? Everyone wants better health, safety and security, love, acceptance and a sense of belonging, growth and financial security and a better overall quality of life. Who would debate the value of these things, and who could say no to any of these things?

Watch how people react when you compare and contrast the inherent benefits of timeshare ownership with these Five Core Motivational Needs. Although everyone wants more of each of these core needs, both individuals and families will prioritize their needs according to their specific situations. Focus on building value around the needs most important to your respective clients. Of these needs, love, acceptance and a sense of belonging appears to be the most dominant for all people. How does timeshare ownership directly generate a sense of love, acceptance and belonging? Over the course of a lifetime, how exactly does the priority associated with these needs change? Tremendous success in sales will be achieved through the proper application of psychological knowledge as it relates to every single client. If timeshare is linked to undeniable needs, then nobody will debate the issues or say no to your product.

If everyone universally wants something and timeshare ownership facilitates and delivers that need, then every client should realize that they should become an owner. Clients will find that they must own timeshare because they will find their lives to be incomplete without it. People will do almost anything to have what they want, and what timeshare has to offer their families. Vacations will no longer be considered a luxury. Vacations are an absolute necessity in this day and age. How many people would like to spend more time with someone special in their lives? Without a doubt, spending quality time with the people someone truly cares about will improve the relationship. This concept cannot be disputed.

When do people truly disconnect from their daily lives and reconnect with their friends, family and loved ones? Normally, it is in conjunction with holidays, weddings, funerals and most importantly, vacations. Vacations represent the essence of quality time, and having more quality time will improve the quality of life for everyone. Therefore, taking more high quality vacations will improve the quality of life. In order to spend more quality time together, people must change their lives and do something different. Change represents the opportunity for growth and the achievement of very basic human needs.

The message inherent to the presentation system, the vital, core needs, will be important to clients from every walk of life. If timeshare is believed to be the catalyst to fulfilling the Five Core Motivational Needs, then what your clients have done in the past will not matter. The future has not been written, and in order to change, people must do something different. Everyone is looking to improve their life, but what is important to one might not be important for another. Don't ever assume anything other than the fact that your clients are going to purchase from you today. Your goal is to show them how ownership at your resort can and will improve their lives. You sell when you believe that your product is superior and will offer the life improvements your clients desire.

Love Life!

"Vacation Ownership enhances *life* by improving relationships."

~ McEneryism

What is most important to you?

Write down the five most important things in your life.

1. _____

2. _____

3. _____

4. _____

5. _____

If you only had six months to live…

Write down the three things you must accomplish before it's over.

1. _____

2. _____

3. _____

Become the Best You Can Be!

Autonomy:

_____

_____

_____

_____

Self Actualization:

_____

_____

_____

_____

What are you willing to give up to achieve Autonomy and Self Actualization? How *bad* do you really want it? How *good* do you really want to become?

Chapter 8

THE DECISION MAKING PROCESS

"*I AM* are the two most powerful words in any language."

The Decision Making Process

When people reflect on their lives, they look at how things are going, and how they want them to be in the future. Because of the fact that people are always striving to grow, there exists a constant drive for change. However, some people are afraid of change. Just because people look to the future doesn't mean they are totally dissatisfied with the present. At any given moment in time, people view their lives with a certain level of satisfaction and acceptance. It is the challenge of timeshare salespeople to have a fundamental knowledge of how people view their lives, and the process clients encounter in association with implementing changes and improvements. People don't want or feel the need to change unless they are either improving their situation for the better or keeping themselves from harm.

Emotions will cause clients to take action much more quickly than logical arguments. In fact, people will go to extreme measures to protect their Five Core Motivational Needs if they feel emotionally motivated. Remember the movie, "John Q." with Denzel Washington where his son would die without an operation, the insurance company wouldn't cover the expense and the hospital refused to provide the operation without money? In order to save his son, Denzel Washington's character held the entire hospital hostage while forcing the doctors to perform the operation. He was willing to suffer the consequences in order to save his son's life. Does this scenario represent a logical decision or an emotional choice?

Human beings will do whatever may be necessary to avoid unpleasant feelings such as grief, remorse, anger or resentment. In extreme situations, people will take action beyond logic in order to protect whatever matters most to them in their lives. Denzel Washington's character chose to take the hospital hostage based upon his feelings. He could not have lived with the remorse and regret associated with taking no action. The emotional dimension of the decision making process always involves seeking pleasure or avoiding pain. The motivation to avoid pain will always dominate over the motivation to seek pleasure.

People make decisions based upon logical sequential thinking and emotional attachment to a situation. Both logic and emotion come into play with every decision, but the emotional dimensions of the decision making process generally prevail in terms of causing people to take action. However, it is the logical aspects of any decision that causes people to stick with their new, consciously chosen direction in life.

The following sections discuss the Emotional Motivators vs. Logical Motivators.

The Emotional Motivator

If someone has an automobile just a few years old, and there is nothing wrong with it aesthetically or mechanically, there exists no immediate reason for them to purchase a new car. Despite the fact that the automobile is just fine and fits the needs of its owner, that person may periodically think about purchasing a new vehicle at some point in the future. If someone came along and offered that person a newer model with more horsepower, better handling and the latest improvements, all for less money, would they be motivated to purchase the new car? Some people would, and some would not. Now, if that person knew that their existing automobile had a serious defect that might cause a wreck impacting the well being of their family members, would that person be more motivated to buy the new car? If someone knew their car had a serious defect and did nothing about it, how would they feel if their decision not to take action seriously hurt their family? What emotions would they feel? Would they have feelings of guilt, remorse, grief and shame? Most people would fix or replace the car prior to a potential wreck in order to avoid these painful emotions.

Every year Americans must file a tax return. They compile their records, itemize their expenses and try to figure out how to complete complicated forms. Most people procrastinate until a certain level of anxiety forces them to take action. Do people go through this stressful process because of the pleasure associated with properly filing their tax return, or do they do it in order to avoid the penalties levied by the government for not filing? It is the avoidance of pain – penalties and tax liens – that keeps people filing their tax returns on a timely basis.

The essence of these examples directly relates to timeshare purchase decisions. Clients may or may not be motivated to save money, or to have extra bells and whistles for their family vacations. They may think in terms of purchasing a vacation ownership plan "someday." However, if they know and understand that the well being of their family is directly related to the ownership of a timeshare, they will be much more motivated to make the purchase and change their lives. The avoidance of pain is a far greater motivator than the hope for gain and pleasure. The brain will go into an action step much more quickly when trying to avoid a painful experience.

People purchase timeshare when they connect with a sense of loss or fear of loss, and believe in the hope for gain. These are emotional motivators, thoughts that will stir up emotions in your clients and cause them to take an action step. You must get them curious enough to consider new possibilities. This is done through putting them in the picture – creating a projection of their future and getting them involved physically, mentally and emotionally in your presentation.

"Selling Timeshare is like Christmas morning. My clients are my presents - I never know what's inside."

~ B. New

"Anything you can tell, you can ask."

~ Tell Seller

"Live in gratitude."

~ U. R. Good

TIMESHARE VACATION MOTIVATORS COMPARATIVE ANALYSIS

PAIN/FEAR OF LOSS

NO VACATIONS

Parental Neglect/Negligence

Spousal Relationship Deterioration

Stagnation/Loss of Adventure

Bad Health/Early Death

No Friends/Poor Family Connections

Loss of Employment

PLEASURE/HOPE FOR GAIN

FREQUENT GREAT VACATIONS

Love/Family/Success/Acceptance

Love/Romance/Sense of Belonging

Growth/Achievement/Excitement

Health/Longevity

Love/Acceptance/Family Relationships

Safety/Security/High Productivity

PAIN/FEAR OF LOSS

NO TIMESHARE OWNERSHIP

Loss of Money/Estate Value

Depression/Lower Quality of Life

Unsafe Environment Spouse/Kids

PLEASURE/HOPE FOR GAIN

FIVE STAR TIMESHARE OWNERSHIP

Growth/Financial Security

Better Quality of Life/Happiness

Safety/Security

PAIN/FEAR OF LOSS

REFUSAL TO MAKE CHANGES

No Growth/Lack of Ambition

Wasted Human Potential/Failure

Procrastinator Guilt/Regret

PLEASURE/HOPE FOR GAIN

ABILITY/WILLINGNESS TO CHANGE

Growth/Achievement/Efficiency

Growth/Better Quality of Life

Happiness/Fulfillment

All people want the same thing. They want to live happy and healthy lives. They want to be reasonably prosperous and have close family relationships. They want hope that the future is going to be better than the past, and they need to know that they have lived a life with purpose and meaning.

Avoidance of Pain / It's in the Story

The use of stories and anecdotes is the most profound way to deliver messages regarding the avoidance of pain or the fear of loss. The stories need to deliver a message relating to the most damaging, painful emotions such as grief, guilt, remorse, regret, shame, humiliation, anger and a sense of failure.

It is vital that you believe and understand this concept. If you don't believe in what timeshare does for the families who are using it, then perhaps you should consider selling a different product. The use of stories is essential to selling timeshare. However, you should carefully plan the timing and frequency of these stories. Since "Avoidance of Pain" and "Fear of Loss" stories are designed to bring forth very powerful negative emotions, once you tell one of these stories you must bring your clients back to the present with resolve to take an action step to eliminate the possibility of experiencing the same problems as the family in your story. People will change when the pain becomes too intense. You must find the pain or create the pain in order to finalize and close a sale. Master Closers find or create a problem, and then link vacation ownership as the solution.

"No Pain, No Gain."

~ Atlas

Seeking Pleasure / Forward Moving Statements

Although people will take action steps significantly more quickly anytime they perceive the opportunity to avoid a painful experience, all sales presentations must also include the potential for gaining pleasure. Forward moving statements serve this purpose by moving clients toward the idea of getting more of the Five Core Motivational Needs in their lives. Since most people want improvement in their lives, they will pay attention to anyone presenting a product or service that will help them accomplish their life goals.

Forward moving statements will capture the attention of your clients, and cause them to listen more closely and participate more actively in the presentation. Your goal is to move your clients from the painful consequences associated with not buying to a positive emotional state realized by achieving ownership. The following statements are highly suggestive with regard to the pleasure associated with acquiring timeshare.

- "If I could show you a way to have better health and rekindle your love while staying in luxury, would you like to hear more about that?"

- "If I could show you a way that people have achieved consistency in quality while securing financial stability with their vacation dollars, would you like to hear more?"

- "If I could show you a way to guarantee your family a happier and healthier lifestyle by staying connected over the years, is there any reason you wouldn't want to know more?"

- "If I could show you a way to stay connected with the people you love while increasing your level of prosperity, would you want to be involved?"

It is important to understand the nuances of human behavior. When you are attempting to explore sensitive subjects with your clients, you must ask for permission. You might ask, "Is it okay if we discuss…?", or "With your permission can we talk about…?", and let it appear that they wish to discuss these issues too. When your clients trust you, they might share a painful memory or a painful moment either past or present, and you will have the opportunity to show them how to avoid similar pain in the future. It is important to use great care when this happens. Be extremely kind and empathetic. Vacation ownership enhances and builds binding relationships. Therefore look for a solution to almost any difficulty through timeshare ownership. Never prejudge that your clients' situation is too dire to consider the idea of ownership. Be firm in your resolve that no matter what your clients' circumstances might be, they will be far better off with ownership than without it. Ownership will, if anything, force people to take vacations. Vacations create memories, and in the end, those memories will be more valuable than any other achievement in life. Life is a series of moments and vacation ownership forces these benefits upon everyone.

Timeshare is not sold in the past or in the present, it is always sold *in the future*. Fear of loss (pain) is always a greater motivator for clients to take an action step toward a same day purchase than hope for gain (pleasure).

Some Emotional Motivators are:

Time with family	Relaxation
Romance	Freedom
Adventure	Quality
Prestige	New experiences
Happiness	Deserving
Legacy	Reconnect with loved ones
Education	Frugal
Realize dreams	Pampering
Quality time	Smart
Love	Safety and security

Acknowledge Pain

Write down something you have done, or a decision you have made, to avoid pain.

_____

_____

_____

_____

_____

_____

_____

_____

_____

_____

_____

_____

Acknowledge Pleasure

Write down something you have done, or a decision you have made, to gain pleasure.

_____

_____

_____

_____

_____

_____

_____

_____

_____

_____

_____

_____

_____

Pain vs. Pleasure

List feelings that would cause pain, and corresponding items in the second column that represent pleasure.

PAIN   **PLEASURE**

The Logical Motivator

Although decisions are primarily based upon emotional connections, there must be some logical rationale behind each decision. When discussing the logical reasons for change, the information must be presented in such fashion that your client perceives change as the logical solution to a problem. The danger associated with logical reasoning lies in the potential to create a debate as to the merits of the proposed change in lifestyle.

Purchasing a timeshare to save money and gain consistent quality in terms of vacation accommodations constitutes a logical statement that could be debated or potentially refuted. However, if the same idea is presented in conjunction with emotional needs common to all human beings, nobody will argue the point. Use emotional need based consensus selling techniques rather than purely logical statements to achieve the highest degree of success in sales.

Predictable Perceptions and Responses

People react to concepts in a variety of ways depending primarily upon the physical context surrounding exposure to the idea, and their personal orientation toward the subject matter based upon life experience. Experts in the field of psychology refer to universally agreed upon empirical perceptions as objectivity, and perceptions filtered through personal opinions and prejudices as subjectivity. Keeping these factors in mind, it is critical to the success of any sales presentation to ask questions and make statements that result in totally predictable perceptions and responses within the heart, body, mind and soul of your clients.

Your goal is to gain agreement to a series of ideas that lead clients to conclude that it is in their best interest to accept the invitation to become involved in a timeshare project as an owner, and to believe that they are joining the program of their own volition. There is great intrinsic value associated with making statements where agreement can be presumed in advance of making the statement, and asking questions that result in predetermined agreement on the part of all clients.

As a sales representative, you must be cognizant of the fact that clients respond to questions and statements both consciously and subconsciously, and that they may acknowledge their agreement or disagreement either verbally or internally. Basing questions and statements upon subject matter pertaining to the Five Core Motivational Needs of all people makes predicting perceptions and responses more of an exact science. As a result, wondering about the impact of questions and statements should never be an issue.

It is difficult in advance to know the response clients might have to general statements like, "You should spend more time with your wife and kids," or "You should take more vacations." Your clients might agree, but they may also think to themselves that they actually do spend plenty of time with their family, and that they take plenty of vacations per year. Your clients could agree or disagree, and may actually become defensive. Below you will find a list of questions which will elicit unpredictable responses:

"You should save more of your money."

"You should travel more because it will benefit your life."

"You should be spending more time with the people you love."

"Your family should be staying in safe places."

"People save money when they buy into a vacation ownership property."

The fundamental idea is to conversationally elicit anticipated favorable responses to questions and statements so that clients can be subtly influenced to having a positive perception of timeshare at the conclusion of your sales presentation. It is important to accomplish this objective without sounding artificial or too polished. Essentially, it is the technique of knowing in advance the reaction or response all clients will have to a specific question or statement. Below, you will find a list of questions that will elicit predictable responses:

"Spending quality time with your loved ones is important, isn't it?"

"Families that travel together stay together."

"Sharing time with the people you love, makes you feel good."

"Times remembered are times shared."

"There is one thing nobody can take away from you and that's your memories."

"As we get older time seems to pass us by, but sometimes we need to slow down so that life doesn't pass us by."

"What holds a marriage together is spending quality time with each other."

"Vacation ownership is about getting more value for your time and money."

"Would you like to have financial stability and security in your lives?"

"Are there people in your life you would like to spend more time with?"

"Would you like to get more value and luxury from the money you are spending?"

"Are there dreams or places yet untraveled?"

"It makes more sense to own than renting your vacations, doesn't it?"

There are undeniable truths that are globally accepted by every human being on Earth. This concept specifically relates to the reinforcement of every person's innate desire to achieve and improve their lives. Every single person in the developed world will have the same response to the rhetorical question, "Do you want your life to have meaning and purpose?" All people will respond in similar favorable fashion to this question. Further, almost anything that can be said as an empirical statement can be asked as a question that will yield a controlled favorable response. Asking people, "Are there loved ones you would like to spend more time with?" or, "Is financial security and independence important to you?" will generate a predictable response.

By causing people to respond and react favorably in a controlled manner to fundamental, implied truths, closing sales will be significantly easier to the point of becoming virtually automatic. An example of an undeniable truth: "The sun is shining today," better phrased… "It is a beautiful day today, isn't it?" This is an example of a tie-down. Tie-downs elicit a "Yes" response – "isn't it?" or "doesn't it?" You must phrase the sentence with something that your clients will answer "Yes" to and then follow with, "isn't it?" If you find your clients nodding or uttering "uh-huh's", coax the word "Yes" from them! The most important part to remember is that as a Master Closer, you are controlling the "Yes" response.

"Your clients will be much better off with timeshare in their lives than without it."

~ B. D. Cisive

"When you're talking, you are controlling the conversation. When you're listening, you are controlling your presentation."

~ McEneryism

Predictable Perception vs. Controlled Responses

Answer the following two questions below as if you were presenting the value of vacations and timeshare.

Finish the following question. Vacations will …

1. _____

2. _____

3. _____

4. _____

5. _____

Finish the following statement. Timeshare will…

1. _____

2. _____

3. _____

4. _____

5. _____

Chapter 9

<u>CONSUMER CONCERNS</u>

"*OBJECTIONS* magically go away when they have no power."

Consumer Concerns

When consumers think about making a buying decision, internally they ask themselves a series of questions about their needs and desires associated with a particular product or service. In other words, they mentally assess if they have a need. Then, they evaluate the expense in terms of time or money in relation to other important decisions in their lives. "I shouldn't buy the boat I have always wanted because we will need a new car next year," or, "We shouldn't be spending this money on vacations because we have to pay for our kids' college in a few years." This thought process occurs in every person, and depending upon individual personalities, your clients may or may not verbalize these thoughts.

One of the most important attributes top performers share is an innate ability to foresee these consumer concerns and to address them before their clients bring them up. Through repetition and continued analysis of your presentations, these consumer concerns become very common with most clients as they determine whether or not to purchase into an ownership program.

For example, your clients may have two children ages 14 and 16, and within a few years, the first one will be going off to college. What thought is most likely going through your clients' minds? "Will we have enough money for our children's college education if we buy this timeshare?" It is important to know and recognize that it is impossible to win when competing against plans people already have in place for their families. Another example might be clients who have very young children, an infant and a two year old. Most likely, they will be thinking that their current traveling will diminish over the next few years, and that it would make better sense to postpone purchasing a timeshare until they start traveling again. How about clients who will be leaving the area soon, and moving to a different state? They will be thinking, "We should hold off until we're settled down into our new home, and then find something nearby." A more common one might be clients who have only stayed in modest hotel rooms. When showing them a beautiful suite, they might be thinking to themselves, "Why should be spend our money on a suite when we are only in the hotel room to sleep? We are always on the go." These thoughts and concerns become very common when your clients evaluate for themselves whether or not they want or need the timeshare product.

Many salespeople try to avoid these common objections by waiting until they are mentioned in the hope that they won't be brought up. However, when the objections are finally verbalized by their clients, these salespeople find themselves in a defensive position where it becomes immediately necessary to acknowledge the objection while presenting an alternative viewpoint on the subject. If your clients have strong feelings about an objection, this approach will cause them to restate and defend their position. Once your clients find themselves in the position of defending an objection, the sale is lost.

Since salespeople can anticipate the most common consumer concerns, it is far more valuable to acknowledge and address the objections prior to the time clients fully consider the objection. This prevents them from becoming entrenched with an adversarial opinion without analyzing the objection from an objective viewpoint. By acknowledging and discussing the most common concerns within your sales presentation, the context of the discussion can be controlled.

If a teenager goes out with some friends, stays out too late and then gets caught sneaking back into the house after an established curfew, how can that child implement damage control and avoid getting into trouble? If the child acknowledges being in trouble, states that he or she should have called home, suggests that the parents should be mad and then presents an explanation, the parents will have very little left to say. By anticipating and acknowledging the concerns any parent would feel in this type of situation, the parents cannot get angry. They have been forced to agree with the child, and all they can do is request that the child call in advance of being late again.

Common consumer concerns include issues such as developer credibility, opportunities on the secondary market, functionality of the exchange system or potential increases in homeowner association dues. Clients sometimes feel that the program presented sounds too good to be true, and many express the desire to shop alternative timeshare developments. Some consumer concerns are more personal such as their perception of the amount of time available for family vacations, or the necessity for quality accommodations. Take a proactive stance, and address these concerns within every presentation.

The art of successfully dealing with consumer concerns is found within the style in which they are handled. The strength when talking about consumer concerns is in the ability to resolve them in an indirect fashion. The use of metaphors, analogies, anecdotes, quotes, current affairs and stories are the best way to deal with these issues.

One of the most important things to understand about dealing with consumer concerns is that you never want to compete against your clients' established position. If someone has a good friend who has told them timeshare is bad, you don't want to say that their friend doesn't know what they are talking about. If your clients enjoy camping or staying with family or friends, don't ask them why or downplay what they are doing in a negative way. Other competing concerns could be your clients' preference for hotel rooms, or their consideration of a second home purchase. The way to handle such concerns is to overlap ownership as an enhancement to what they are already doing. Millions of people do exactly what these clients are doing, and have vacation ownership in their lives. When people want to stay in luxury surroundings and have a truly magnificent vacation, they use timeshare.

When your clients give you a reason why they will not purchase, you must discern whether this is an objection or a condition. An objection is a "Not yet," and a condition is a "We can't." You can overcome any objection, even "We can't afford it." When someone states they can't afford your product, they may just be saying "We don't see the value in your product *yet*." Now, if they truly are broke, that is a condition and *usually* cannot be overcome. But remember, if the emotion and desire is strong enough, the objections will go away and, at times, so will the conditions. Those conditions that *appear* to be standing in the way of a sale need to be thoroughly explored.

Perception is reality.

Objections vs. Conditions

Objection: A feeling or expression of opposition

Condition: A general state or mode of existence, especially one characterized by hardship or suffering.

Some objections:

"We don't believe it works the way you say it does."
"It doesn't make financial sense for us."
"It seems too complicated."
"It doesn't fit our lifestyle."

Some conditions:

"We can't afford it."
"We don't take vacations."
"We don't have good health."
"We wouldn't use it."

Sympathy: The *ability to enter into*, or share somebody else's feelings.

Empathy: The ability to identify with and *understand* somebody else's feelings or difficulties.

As a salesperson, you want to have empathy for your clients' problems, never sympathy! There is a critical distinction between the two. Picture yourself in a boat in the ocean when all of a sudden you see another boat come along side that is taking on water and sinking quickly. If you had sympathy for the passengers of the other boat, you would jump into their boat with them; if you had empathy for them, you would throw them a life vest and rope and help them into your boat. When your clients tell you what their problems are – we don't vacation, or our kids' sports take all our time and money, his job keeps him too busy, etc. – you want to help them solve their problems or get them out of their sinking boat. If you accept their excuses you are just jumping in with them. Sympathy changes *your* emotional state; it causes you to take on emotions such as sorrow, anger or resentment. Empathy changes *their* emotional state; it offers them happiness, relief or hope. There is a sale made at every presentation. Either you sold them or they sold you.

Wonderful

An owner approached me and one of our sales brokers, Randall Grimm, while we were both standing at the front desk. She forcefully approached me and demanded an answer, "Do you remember me?" Unfortunately, I did not immediately recognize her so I said, "Could you please give me some information about yourself?" She said, "I am Marcia Smith, and my husband, Henry, and I became owners with you about five years ago." I said, "Tell me more!" She said "We're from New Jersey and we love Colorado!" I said, "A*nd?*" Marcia replied, "Remember Henry? He was the white-haired, skinny guy who was really frail." I said, "Now I remember!" She said, "He had cancer and it wasn't looking too good for him back then." I looked at her with grave concern and she replied, "Oh, I forgot to say, he's alive and doing great! I want to thank you so much for not giving up on us and doing such a magnificent job. Because of your patience and persistence, Henry and I travelled all throughout Europe, on a five-week timeshare vacation to Italy, France, Spain and Portugal. We just came back from your In-House Sales department and upgraded our ownership!" They had purchased more timeshare! Marcia and I exchanged warm welcomes and a big hug as long lost friends would have experienced. Randall Grimm, one of our top brokers, was standing there in amazement. I definitely could see the joy he was experiencing by witnessing such an impactful life moment. I truly believe that if I had prejudged the situation and dismissed those clients because of sympathy, it would have been a huge mistake and an injustice. Therefore, when presenting your product, *always live in empathy.*

Empathize with your clients and solve their problems with the features and benefits of your product, then of course, turn the product into features, advantages and benefits. What if your clients don't think they have a problem? Make one for them! When Moms and Dads live to work there is a disconnect with a strong family relationship. Working too much triggers ill health. No vacation time together causes strife between family members and leads to divorce. Now that your clients have problems they didn't realize they had, you can solve them with the benefits of your product.

An effective trust-building response to an objection is to genuinely smile, pause for a moment, and say "How do you mean, exactly?" Then, follow up with a Third Party Story where you are placing someone else as the focal point of the discussion and telling someone else's experience rather than your own. As simple as it sounds, a third party story is not about you. A third party story must be credible and relevant, and must reflect a similar family situation to that of your clients. You should also have a positive outcome every time. You want to say how the others' situation was the same, how they felt, and what they found once they became owners of your product.

For example: "Bob and Mary, I understand how you *feel*. I have some owners, John and Susan in Denver, who *felt* the same way you do. Once they started using this product, though, they *found* that...." Of course you fill in the details of the situations and circumstances for any specific issue.

What you have done is acknowledge that Bob and Mary have a valid concern, and one that has been expressed before by other clients. Then you have shown how your product solved whatever issue was at hand. Bob and Mary can project their lives into your story, and now they can imagine a better life just like John and Susan are enjoying, exclusively as a result of owning your product.

There are rules and there are laws. The law of a third party story is to always use a Compliance Trial Close or a Commitment Trial Close immediately after telling your third party story. (These closing techniques are explained in Chapter 10.) The sole purpose is to earn trust and close. You have earned the right to Trial Close because a great third party story takes tremendous effort on your part. A third party story does not have the word "I" in it. It is about somebody else because people believe stories about others. The best-selling book globally is the Bible. The Bible is all third party stories. Success is usually not invented. It is just copied. Don't reinvent the wheel.

The definition of a *condition* has hardship and suffering within its meaning. Therefore, most salespeople will feel sorry for or sympathize with their clients' condition. This is not uncommon. It's just inappropriate for a salesperson to judge that their clients should not purchase for whatever reason. Always *inspire*. Live and work *in spirit*. Always perform your very best presentation, and let the chips fall where they may. You just might change and enhance your clients' lives.

When challenged with a condition, use the "Feel, Felt, Found" technique. You, the salesperson, should live and stay in empathy and understanding. Pick a condition, and use this method. For example, "We don't vacation"…

_____

_____

What should you do after a third party story? Commitment Trial Close! "Can I get you started with our program here today?" A Master Closer would expect a "No", meaning "Not yet, I need more information," and continue on. The most common consumer concerns are separated by the two categories of clients. Each category will have similar, but different concerns.

Non-Timeshare Owner

Time Objection

The time objection is one that needs to be covered because people have very hectic, fast paced lifestyles. Many feel they will not have the time to go anyplace. This is obvious when clients have had only one vacation in many years. One of them may be a workaholic, or starting a new job. They may be moving, or have young children. They may be facing major life changes. You need to either have your clients acknowledge that they don't want the past to continue into the future, or with a crafted example or two, show them that their issues associated with not having the time to vacation are not reality.

Money Objection

When it comes down to it, not being able to justify the expenditure of the money it takes to vacation is the number one reason people don't go on vacation. This concern is even greater than not having the time to vacation and will be apparent when your clients only stay in modest places, or have kids going off to college. It will also be apparent when your clients are buying a new house, changing jobs or only stay with family and friends. Money objections should be covered in the RENT VS. OWN section of your presentation. Get your clients to acknowledge that regardless of whatever expenses they may have in their lives, their desire to spend quality time together is of the utmost importance. Your clients must also acknowledge the fact that they have been, and will continue to spend the money anyway. Show your clients what the cost will be if they don't change the way they spend their money. Convince them that every dollar spent in the past, and the money they are going to spend in the future on vacations will truly enhance and benefit their lives on a long term basis. Having clients justify past expenses also yields an understanding of their financial stability.

Life's Expenses

Many people live paycheck to paycheck, and don't have any surplus money for things like vacations. In fact, they may view vacations as a luxury that they would enjoy, but cannot justify or afford. They are spending everything they have on the expenses of life. These are the families extended to the limit. This objection can be transparent or very difficult to see, and it is not success specific. Your clients could be making a lot of money, but remain extended to the limit. They could also be in a more modest income bracket with limited cash availability. This concern encompasses all of life's expenses such as having kids going off to college, building a house, having to buy a new car, changing jobs or being out of work. If these people don't start making changes to the manner in which they spend their discretionary income and start investing more, their financial future will be impaired.

Developer Credibility

Developer credibility more commonly arises as a concern with first time buyers that have never before attended a timeshare presentation. They bring up the concern, "We will need to do some research before committing to a purchase." Other concerns which arise from this are, "How do we know that we will be able to use the program in the manner in which it has been presented?" They may also be thinking, "Why should we buy this program instead of some other program?"

Timeshare Credibility

The history of timeshare has not been without its trials and tribulations. The damage this industry inflicted upon itself and its reputation in its early years is still around today. This concern can appear if your clients know someone who owns, or have family members who own. Because people will always trust their friends and family first over some salesperson, it will be important to share how the industry has changed over the years, and how your product is different. Changing the perception of your clients can be done by explaining that no two products are exactly the same, and that just because some other program has not met the expectations of someone else, doesn't mean that the entire product or industry is bad. Expressing the challenges of the timeshare industry illustrates the imperfection of this industry and every other business in an honest way. Remember, the product doesn't have to be perfect, it only has to be better than the alternative.

It's Only a Room

This consumer concern appears when your client is only willing to pay a modest price for vacation accommodations. They choose to justify what they get because they are not willing to part with more money. This concern appears in statements like, "We don't spend much time in the room so the room is not important to us." They may also say, "We enjoy camping" or "We enjoy staying with family and friends." Show your clients that this thought doesn't reflect their true feelings. People will always take more for less if the opportunity presents itself. People will say that the room doesn't matter to them, but they really don't mean it.

The Product Doesn't Meet Lifestyle Objectives

Because timeshare has been predominately purchased in weekly increments, consumers who take shorter vacations because of either time or money restrictions will feel the product doesn't fit their needs. Consumers discussing travel in Europe may say that they prefer to cover a lot of territory, and that a week long stay would be restrictive. Overcome this concern by explaining that timeshare has the ultimate flexibility of both size of accommodations and length of stay through innovative points programs. Through the First Day Incentives offered at your resort, your clients will be able to use their deeded time at their home resort for shorter stays with Bonus Time or an internal points program. Owners still take mini vacations to relieve stress and anxiety from their daily lives. However, when it's time to connect with family and friends in a luxurious setting, sometimes it is a week long stay that becomes the vacation of choice. Today's timeshare programs can provide for either scenario.

It is important to limit your explanation of points until it is clear that your clients have a need to know more. Spilling all the ins and outs of a complicated system can be very confusing to anyone, and your purpose is simply to express the flexibility of ownership with your resort. (Keep It So Simple = K.I.S.S.) Your sole purpose is to keep your presentation and explanations simple, easy and fun. Remember, your job is to sell, not to teach. Many timeshare agents are teachers, and as a result, are always at the bottom of the wheel. Those who insist on being teachers ultimately either starve out or are asked to resign by management. A great habit to implement and remember: "Anything you can say, you can ask".

The System Doesn't Work

One of the main concerns regarding timeshare ownership is the fact that many people have heard that it just doesn't work. As a result, some people have the perception that the systems in place will not meet their expectations. This objection can be transparent, or difficult to recognize. One indicator may be family or friends who own but haven't had a positive experience. If your clients are more affluent, their freedom in terms of scheduling can be a very big concern. Address this concern in the PRODUCT portion of the presentation when explaining the exchange and how your reservations system works. During the PRODUCT portion of your presentation, it is very important to pay attention to the receptiveness of your clients in terms of body language including facial expressions and their eyes. These signs reveal whether or not they understand or believe what they are hearing. Also pay attention to the quantity and quality of the questions they ask. If they ask no questions, there will be no sale.

Use baby negatives while explaining the product, and honestly share with every client what the product will not do. A baby negative is the disclosure of a small problem with your product, one that is not very consequential. For example, "You won't always get the exact resort or location you want, but you'll get pretty close," or "You probably won't get Christmas or New Year's in a highly demanded ski area. Is that okay?" The use of baby negatives at key points within your presentation only strengthens the consumer's belief in what you are selling because they know that nothing is perfect. The biggest mistake timeshare salespeople make is pitching an imperfect product as perfect. Therefore, clients will often say at the end of the presentation, "This is too good to be true. I want to think about it." A Master Closer who gets the "too good to be true" *during* his presentation simply overcomes this objection. When asked "This sounds too good to be true. What's the downside?" the Master Closer will enthusiastically state "The worst thing that could happen would be for you to purchase an ownership interest today and then not use it." Your clients will always respond "If we did purchase, of course we would use it!" Exactly! Timeshare doesn't have to be perfect, just better than your clients' current vacation lifestyle.

HOA Dues

It has been said the number one reason people don't purchase into a timeshare development is the ongoing liability associated with the homeowner association dues. This is the one expense associated with timeshare ownership that will never end, and people think that if the system does not meet their expectations that they will be affected financially in a negative way. Since this one is a concern for all, when speaking about maintaining the quality of the resort, automatically let your clients know that the homeowner association dues will continue to change over the course of time. This is the best money your new owners will ever spend because it ensures that their resort will be properly maintained and kept in five star, premiere condition.

Resale

The timeshare industry has been plagued with mediocre products and oversaturated developments that have hurt the residual value of timeshare ownerships. It can be difficult, but not impossible to sell a timeshare on the secondary market, and most people are aware of this fact. To address this issue, use the same idea associated with purchasing a car out of the paper versus purchasing from a dealership. It is usually cheaper to purchase on the secondary market, but most people prefer to buy from the developer or a dealership. Price, in most cases, is not the most important consideration. Service and support after the sale tend to weigh heavier because people want someone backing the product they have purchased. This concern can also be difficult to uncover because most of the time people do not want to admit to this line of thinking. The challenges presented by the resale market generally impact the front end closing percentage much more than they affect rescission rates. When dealing with this objection, acknowledge that there are many ways to buy timeshare, but point out the value of doing business with the developer. Place high value on the personal relationship between yourself and your clients. Without creating a new objection, try to get your clients to acknowledge their level of familiarity with the resale market, and get them to bring it up so that this objection can be addressed in a positive manner. Emphasize that it is more important to have full support and service than just a price discount. Usually, in today's environment, there are features and benefits unique to the developer/client relationship that do not transfer on the resale market. These features and benefits, generally first day incentives that are non-transferable, should be reiterated and emphasized if resale is presented as an objection. Therefore, you must build value around these exclusive unique benefits.

"When you're not selling, you're not selling. A sale is made every day. Either you sold them or they sold you."

~ A. Lesson

Timeshare Owner

Developer Credibility

All timeshare owners have either had a great experience with a developer and would only want to buy more from them, or they have had a bad experience with ownership and don't believe anything will change.

Bad Experience

When owners express feelings about bad experiences, it is usually associated with the exchange or the overall operation of the program. They tend to feel nothing will change or be different from their previous experience. When this concern is prevalent, it is important find out some additional information. How long have your clients owned timeshare, and where do they own? What type of ownership do they have? Is it points or weeks? Then acknowledge that timeshare is not perfect, but point out that many things have changed and improved over the years. Share the importance of proactive customer service as a culture within your company.

Good Experience

When owners have had a good experience with timeshare, it can take two forms. They may own a high profile timeshare with a brand name, and don't think any resort without a brand name can match that experience. They may also have purchased at a resort that sells for less money than the one being presented, and as a result feel that if they would ever consider purchasing additional time, they would go back and purchase more time at their first resort. Once again, find out some more information. Present your resort as unique and different, and emphasize the company's dedication to service and support after the sale.

Time Objection / Too Many Weeks

When consumers own several programs, it is not uncommon for them to feel that they own enough time. Deal with this concern by establishing the fact that the amount of time these clients currently own will not be enough in the future. Talk about the fact that as time goes on, people tend to travel more, not less. Investing is not an event, but a process. Having additional time in place will create more security for the future. If your clients are not fully utilizing their current ownership, they must be convinced that they will use and greatly enjoy another week, and be given suggestions as to alternative uses for their other weeks.

Money Objection

Many times, timeshare owners feel that if they were to consider purchasing another timeshare, they would need to sell one of their other weeks first. Discuss this point by asking a very direct question, "If you fell in love with this ownership and were considering purchasing here today, would you keep the weeks you already have or would you consider selling one of them first?" Many times, your clients will say that they would keep what they already have, but at the very end of the tour they will lay down the trump card and say, "We like this program, but we would have to sell one of our weeks before purchasing." Keep the price high until this comes out. This issue might come up because they like the product you are presenting better than their current ownership, and now just don't want the other one. However, it could be that they just don't want to pay association dues on multiple weeks. Money becomes a strong consideration with moderate income clients.

HOA Dues

The liability associated with additional dues keeps many owners from purchasing more time. This is especially true if they have not received the value they expected the first time around. Justifying another association bill will not make sense to these people. In this instance, it will be vitally important to create additional value for your timeshare product. Assure your clients that continuing to invest in the future is the only road to financial stability.

Resale

Over the course of time, owners learn about the secondary market, and the fact that it is cheaper than purchasing from a developer. However, it is always better to purchase from the developer because of service and benefit considerations. Find out if your clients have received great value from their ownership, and find out how they originally purchased. Ask them, "If you were to do it over again, what would you change, if anything?"

Buying Signals

Buying signals can be obvious or extremely subtle. Watch for changes in facial expressions and gestures. Direct eye contact and a smile can signal a desire to make a purchase. Clients holding hands, or looking at one another and nodding demonstrate engagement in the sales process and an understanding of the benefits to be derived from making a purchase. Active participation in the sales discussion and positive interaction with the sales materials shows interest. Pay attention, and take advantage of these moments by asking for the sale when clients are eliciting positive buying signals. You must stay focused and always be *in the zone* to recognize buying signals.

Objections

Consumer concerns represent broad issues consumers face when making a decision to purchase. Consumer concerns may or may not be verbalized through the course of a presentation. However, objections are more specific - direct questions or statements made by consumers regarding the product or associated financial conditions.

Throughout the sales presentation, focus on keeping the end result in mind – getting to the final "Yes" and consummating the sale. Continually watch for buying signals which may be verbal or more subtle such as shifts in body language or tone of voice. Objections often reveal buyer interest, but must be handled diplomatically. Trail closes should be used to determine your clients' level of interest and commitment. It is vital to gain incremental commitments from clients throughout every sales presentation. Without commitment, the presentation will end with a polite, "Thank you", and be void of any agreement to purchase.

You must diplomatically address objections using a variety of techniques as outlined below.

Set Aside: Consumers frequently have questions or concerns that may appear to be relevant to the decision making process. However, more often than not, these are questions asked for purposes of clarification that do not require further explanation. Set aside negative questions or statements as irrelevant and unimportant unless your clients repeat them. Only then should you address them as being relevant to the sales process.

Paraphrase for Clarity: When an objection is poorly stated and the question is vague, you should paraphrase and restate the question so that your response is specific to the concern.

Agree: Sometimes, client objections are relevant and true. In this case, you should agree with your clients, and acknowledge the issue with empathy. Admitting shortcomings associated with the product gains credibility, and demonstrates a personal level of understanding. Your clients will feel your honesty, and appreciate the level of integrity inherent to the entire sales process. Simply acknowledge that no product is perfect, then emphasize that timeshare is different, and highlight how it is better than any alternative in the travel product marketplace.

Make It Worse: Another effective way of dealing with objections is to make the situations worse. For example, if your clients have teenage children and the cost of college comes into play, tell them that their kids will probably be in school no longer than 10 or 12 years depending upon the number of graduate degrees they decide to pursue. Then ask them if they are willing to put their lives on hold for that length of time. Very often, they will look at the issue of college tuition as a relatively minor four year commitment rather than a major stumbling block. Humor sells vacation ownership!

Trial Closes: Trial closes are essential to the success of every sales presentation. Ask your clients early and often about the functionality and relevance of the product and associated benefits. Trial closes serve to confirm participatory engagement on the part of your clients, and should be phrased so as to lead them to the conclusion that timeshare will truly enhance their leisure lifestyle. Trial closes should also be used to isolate and confirm the right season, unit size, and frequency of use to be recommended in the PRODUCT portion of the presentation.

Avoid cliché Trial Closes and Tie-Downs such as "You can see how this would benefit your family, can't you?" Instead, ask direct straight forward buying questions related to the core features and benefits of the product, and then connect those questions with the issue of making a buying decision today. For example, "If you were to become owners here today, what size residence would work best for your family?" "As our newest owners, where will you go and what will you do with your family on your next vacation?"

Dismissing Objections

At times, as a seasoned Master Closer, you can use the phrase, "other than that...", or not acknowledge an objection and move past it. This is quite an effective technique. This is where you amp it up, continue to sell and assume the sale. If your clients say, "We don't do anything the same day," you disregard that statement and say with enthusiasm, "Other families just like yours love being owners with us!" Then link their emotional motivator to your product and say, "they wanted to spend valuable and fun time snowboarding with their kids, just like you do!" People only hear and recall seven percent of your words, so your body language and tonality must display excitement, exhilaration, passion and conviction. Standing Ovation.

Even if your clients say, "You haven't heard me, we're not doing it today," in your mind the "Not today" means "Not yet," "We need more information," and "You haven't sold us yet." Your clients are saying to you, "Please sell us a timeshare today." If you truly believe this message, why would you stop and acknowledge something that is not real? If this technique is too powerful for you, you could start your statement with "No big deal..." and eventually take this statement out when you become more confident.

Remember, sales is just a game. When you are playing a game you truly love, you always want to win. The game becomes like chess where you are thinking so many moves ahead, you always expect to win. Winning means that you are victorious in securing vacation moments and memories for your clients to share with one another and their loved ones. When you have the wisdom and courage to act decently bold and you are truly selling from "your heart of hearts" in attempting to help your clients, what else could be better? *Go out on the skinny branches because that's where the fruit is.* Now and only in the present moment can you summon up the spirit to do what it takes to become the "Greatest Of All Time." Many clients leave a timeshare presentation without an owners' book because they have encountered an *unprepared* salesperson. After reading this book, never say, "Oh, I couldn't possibly do that," because someone who is willing to "do that" will take your place. Understand that it is not difficult to become great. It is difficult to stay great. You must have the strength, passion and conviction to push through any obstacle. You were hired for your competitiveness and you must win, so that your clients will win!

Remember, you have been spoon fed through self help books, educational systems, parents, guidance counselors and peers to believe that "Knowledge is Power," which is a false statement. Knowledge is not power. You need action for anything to become a power.

"Knowledge plus *Action* equals Power"

~ McEneryism

"Even if he fails again and again to accomplish his purpose (as he necessarily must until weakness is overcome) the strength of character gained will be the measure of his true success, and this will form a starting point in his life for future power and triumph."

~ James Allen

What objections would you dismiss?

_____

_____

_____

_____

_____

_____

Why did you choose those particular objections to dismiss?

_____

_____

_____

_____

_____

_____

Overcome the Consumer Concerns

Write down consumer concerns that are relevant to your client and to your resort and how you would overcome those issues/problems.

1. Developer Credibility:

   _____

   _____

   _____

2. Time Objection:

   _____

   _____

   _____

3. Justify the Money:

   _____

   _____

   _____

4. Timeshare Credibility:

_____

_____

_____

5. Life's Expenses:

_____

_____

_____

6. It's Only a Room:

_____

_____

_____

7. The System Doesn't Work:

_____

_____

_____

8. HOA Dues:

_____

_____

_____

9. Resale:

_____

_____

_____

"Whatsoever a man soweth, that shall he also reap."

~ Galatians 6: 7-9 (KJV)

"To be the best you must do the hard work."

~ V. Elocity

Role Play

Role playing can be a fun and entertaining way to perfect your craft. Pair up with someone and have one person be the client and the other the salesperson. Pick the most common objections and conditions you encounter. First attempt to dismiss the objections and conditions, then overcome them with passion and conviction.

Use this exercise as practice because you always get a second chance to improve your methods toward *perfect practice*.

_____

_____

_____

_____

_____

_____

<u>Perfect practice!</u>

Never practice in the game.
Practice with a *successful* partner.
Your presentation is the game.

Chapter 10

TRIAL CLOSING TECHNIQUES

"ASK and you shall receive."

Trial Closing Techniques

There are two types of trial closing questions: Compliance Trial Closes and Commitment Trial Closes.

Compliance Trial Closing

Compliance trial closing techniques are used when you need to be non-threatening. Use these techniques when your client might be frustrated or unenthusiastic, or worse, angered, nasty or combative. A compliance technique is used when you refer to someone else. Fortunately, when this technique is used, you can test the waters without upsetting your client. You never want to pour gasoline on a fire! If you said, "You should buy this," it might cause a fight or flight response rather than simply stating, "Do you see why we have so many owners?"

Compliance Trial Closes using "our owners" or "they," are designed to build your relationship with your clients and to get a *yes* momentum, such as:

"Can you see why our owners love this?"

"Do you see why our Club Benefits are so popular with our owners?"

Compliance Stories are amazing Third Party Stories about your owners using all of the five senses. Pick up any magazine, and read the advertisements because their ad executives get paid millions of dollars to sell in color. When you sell in color, you will need to use all the five senses with great passion and vibrant adjectives. Remember, to inspire your clients you must always be "in-spirit!"

Commitment Trial Closing

Commitment Trial Closing techniques are used when you have successfully increased the buying pressure incrementally, whereas your clients are putting themselves in the picture because you have respectfully kept them out of the picture until they wanted it. This is when and where your clients start to tune into their favorite radio station WIIFM (What's In It For Me), and you have recognized subtle hints that they are considering what you are offering. Clients will say, "Please tell me about the Day Use again," or "If we buy this today, do we get the Day Use?" A great follow-up to those questions is "Bob and Mary, I want to ask you about the Day Use. I just want to clarify and confirm, so that you and I understand how the Day Use privilege works (reiterate how it works). Bob and Mary, do you understand how the Day Use works? Any other questions? Most importantly, I must ask you, do you remember how you get the Day Use?" Be sure at this exact moment you remain completely silent and wait for however long it takes, no matter how uncomfortable the silence may be, for them to respond, "To get the Day Use we would need to buy today." "Perfect. Are you more prepared to do that now than you were earlier in our presentation?"

It is important to clarify and make sure your clients understand that by TODAY you mean during their initial visit - which ends after their tour. This will prevent them from asking, "What time do you leave today?" and thinking that by First Day, you mean the end of the business day. Today *always* means Initial Visit!

You must be connected and on the same page as your clients so that they trust you, like you and truly believe that ownership at your resort will be an asset and a benefit in their lives. You must learn to not use commitment techniques too soon because your clients will view you as a salesperson rather than a counselor and their newest best friend. Master Closers usually describe their new owners in the day-after sales meetings by saying, "I met some really nice people!" because all parties felt the love.

Commitment Trial Closes, using "you" and "your family", are designed to uncover objections and the "not today" issue, such as:

"Am I possibly looking at my newest owners?"

"If you bought this today would you....?"

Closing techniques are not just the final step. That is why you Trial Close before the CLOSE (the last step in the 12 STEPS TO SUCCESS). Your intention is to always Trial Close and test the waters before the final CLOSE. You should be Compliance Trial Closing and Commitment Trial Closing right after the INTENT TO SELL (step 5 in the 12 STEPS TO SUCCESS). Study and master Compliance and Commitment Trial Closes. It is an essential piece of the puzzle, and it is the most important technique of the sales process. You must learn to seamlessly transition and switch in a moment's notice between Compliance and Commitment Trial Closes. Watch your clients' body language. When they are becoming resistive, it is because you are using Commitment Trial Closes too early or too often. Therefore, you are not being fully aware, and you must correct this immediately. A Master Closer effortlessly switches back to Compliance Trial Closes when tension, negative energy or negative body language become apparent. Mastering this sales technique maintains trust so all of your hard work is not lost.

With practice you will develop unconscious competence (using your knowledge without thinking about it) to transition between Compliance and Commitment Trial Closes – knowing when to move forward or back off a bit based on your clients' reactions and responses to your questions. You must study your clients' body language to understand when you're pushing too hard. This is where you switch from Commitment Trial Closes back to Compliance Trial Closes.

"Discernment is the quality of being able to grasp and comprehend what is obscure. Keenly selective judgment."

~ Webster

"I know, that I know, that I know"

~ McEneryism

Compliance vs. Commitment Trial Closes

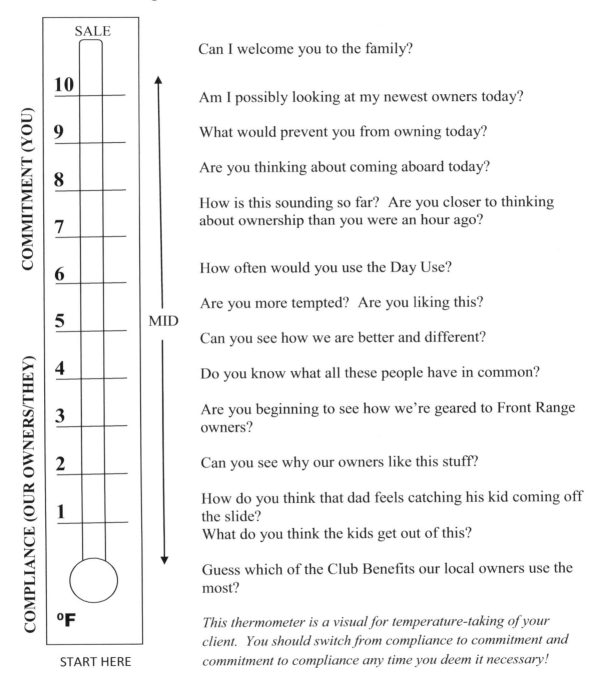

Can I welcome you to the family?

Am I possibly looking at my newest owners today?

What would prevent you from owning today?

Are you thinking about coming aboard today?

How is this sounding so far? Are you closer to thinking about ownership than you were an hour ago?

How often would you use the Day Use?

Are you more tempted? Are you liking this?

Can you see how we are better and different?

Do you know what all these people have in common?

Are you beginning to see how we're geared to Front Range owners?

Can you see why our owners like this stuff?

How do you think that dad feels catching his kid coming off the slide?
What do you think the kids get out of this?

Guess which of the Club Benefits our local owners use the most?

This thermometer is a visual for temperature-taking of your client. You should switch from compliance to commitment and commitment to compliance any time you deem it necessary!

Chapter 11

ACTION INHIBITORS

"*PROCRASTINATORS* are made, not born."

Action Inhibitors

The tendency for people to procrastinate must be addressed in every presentation. Procrastination is unproductive, the downfall of dynamic, successful people. Everyone lives within a certain finite dimension of familiarity, and moving out of that "Comfort Zone" can cause a significant amount of consternation. Unless clients feel an immediate need to change their lives, they will typically postpone initiating change because people are generally afraid of change. They are afraid they can't handle it, and afraid of making a bad decision.

According to the philosopher Charles Kettering, "The world hates change, yet change is the only thing that has ever brought progress." It is critical that your clients acknowledge the fact that growth and improvements in life cannot be accomplished without change. The more a proposed change can be directly linked to the Five Core Motivational Needs of all human beings, the more likely clients will embrace the idea of making a change in their lives.

Regardless of whether or not the issue is formally addressed, all human beings feel afraid of the unknown. This constitutes an important component of the idea of the fear of change. Although everyone feels fear associated with the unknown, not everyone is consciously aware as to why they have those feelings. Many people will question their ability to handle a proposed change. By coaching and telling stories associated with the issues surrounding change, clients must be convinced that they will rise to the occasion of handling change in their lives.

Many people experience a form of paralysis when it comes to making a decision. They may have made an impulsive decision at some point in their lives that they later regretted. Some people go so far as to make it a policy to avoid immediate decisions at any cost. Remember, decisions that move people toward fulfillment will be much more palatable than decisions peripheral to those needs. It is important to emphasize within the context of every presentation the fact that being indecisive can be very detrimental to a person's happiness and well being.

The act of making decisions is what moves people forward in their lives. Some choices in life may initially appear to be bad decisions, but later turn out to be the direct cause of excellent, unanticipated results. In the 1950's, Ford Motor

Company launched a new model called the Edsel. This new model quickly became a joke, the poorest performing model in the history of automotive sales. Ford Motor Company lost significant amounts of money designing and developing the Edsel, yet the technological advances discovered in conjunction with those design endeavors later gave birth to the Ford Mustang – the most successful line of cars in automotive history.

Although not every decision proves to be a good decision, it is vital to continue making decisions in order to succeed in life. Sometimes, people lose money in the stock market. If someone decided to never make another investment ever again as a result of making a bad one, would that person have the opportunity to enjoy much in the way of financial security in the future? Thomas Edison conducted more than a thousand tests in his efforts to design a light bulb. When later asked about those experiments, he said, "I successfully made all those tests in order to learn what to do." The greatest irony is the fact that making no decision is still a decision. When reviewing decisions made over a lifetime, people are more likely to regret missed opportunities than failed initiatives.

Always discuss the issues surrounding decision making in a non-aggressive fashion. Third Party Stories, quotations, anecdotes, metaphors, and humor are the most effective methods associated with delivering information to clients concerning the need to make changes in their lives. It is important to touch upon as many of the core human needs and action inhibitors as possible during the course of a sales presentation in order for clients to connect with the information. Clients must internally subscribe to the ideas presented, and feel a compelling need to change the way they have been living in order for positive changes to begin in their lives.

People have a tendency to procrastinate, and put off decisions they feel are not immediate needs. The core of the presentation is designed to move customers away from procrastination, and into taking an Action Step. If they put off making a decision, the consequences might be too great if something tragic were to happen. This concept becomes the underlying theme of the presentation. You never get back today, and tomorrow may never come. You never know when something can happen to make you completely rethink your life. Do you want the pain associated with looking back over your life, and thinking to yourself, "Has my life been completely wrong? Have I had the wrong focus on life itself, and now I cannot get back what would have been so precious to me?"

There are three Action Inhibitors which should be understood in order to give your clients an understanding that tomorrow may never come, and that you can't get back yesterday. The three are: Fear of Change, Fear They Can't Handle It, and Fear of Making a Bad Decision.

Fear of Change

The Fear of Change is a condition that affects all decisions. Unless your clients are open and become willing to change, they will not take an Action Step. You need to have your clients acknowledge the fact that in order for them to get more of what they want in life, they need to change how they have been doing things.

The Fear of Change relates to the common Consumer Concerns within each category. Take a look back at the Consumer Concerns. Each one of them deals with initiating change from what your clients have been previously accustomed to doing. Buying into ownership, or adding additional weeks, is a change from what they have been doing.

Fear They Can't Handle It

At the root of procrastination is the fear they can't handle it. All fears really come down to this very basic, common feeling. People think to themselves, "If I make a bad decision, will I be able to handle the embarrassment of it?" They also think, "If I take on another payment, can I support the debt load?" In reality, everyone has made decisions that have not panned out. Everyone has taken on more than they could handle. Everyone has walked into the unknown, and come out okay. No matter what has happened in the past, or will happen in the future, people can handle it. Think about your own past experiences, and some of the situations you have gotten into, and survived. Today, as you read this, are you okay?

Fear of Making a Bad Decision

People will put off making a decision if they feel it might be a bad decision. However, if the decision moves them toward the Five Core Motivational Needs, how could it be bad? The reason this fear exists is because of the fact that as we go through life, we will have made some choices that just didn't pan out as initially envisioned. Some people might label the choice as a failure, while others would consider it necessary for success. Everyone has some degree of failure in life.

"I want to think about it is a *stall tactic* meaning
I need more information. I am not ready yet."

"Making no decision is still a decision."

"Purpose is something set up as an end to be attained. A goal of an action intentionally undertaken. Resolution, determination."

"Sell and Close with Purpose."

~ McEneryism

Chapter 12

EFFECTIVE COMMUNICATION TECHNIQUES

"Become a great *LISTENER*."

Effective Communication Techniques

Passion represents the single most important ingredient of a sales presentation. Think of the passion associated with the delivery of a Sunday morning sermon in a Southern Baptist church. Based upon faith and emotional conviction, preachers speak about life principles and undeniable truths with the express purpose of reaffirming faith in the congregation and recruiting new church members.

There is a correlation between that preacher's sermon and your timeshare presentation. Parables in the Bible are third party stories. Great stories represent the most dynamic way to convey a message because stories can present a moral principle or some other persuasive point without being confrontational. Every sales presentation should be filled with a number of short stories designed to make crucial points in a non-confrontational manner.

There should be two types of stories in every sales presentation, those directly related to the timeshare product, and those about general life experiences. Tasteful humor should also be integrated into every presentation. Clients should enjoy the presentation, and be totally relaxed in order to feel comfortable with the idea of making a purchase. Humor can provide a great deal of assistance toward the achievement of these goals.

Third Party Stories should be used in the WHY VACATION portion of the presentation to create emotional pain. Clients must feel the pain associated with procrastination in order to feel urgency to make a change in their lives. Both first and third party stories should be used in conjunction with descriptions of the exchange system in order to establish the quality of the exchange network, and demonstrate the functionality of the system.

By definition, effective communication is the transference of mental and emotional energy. The actual words spoken during the course of a sales presentation barely matter given the fact that they represent an extremely minute portion of the overall communications process. It is the physical delivery of those words that makes the difference. However, avoid using words that you don't want your clients to repeat back to you, like "interesting," "informative," "learning," "probably," or "maybe." Remember, work smart and always be decently bold!

Every human being emanates attitude and emotion on a variety of conscious and subconscious levels. The ability to deliver passion, inspiration, excitement and hope will ultimately determine the effectiveness of every sales representative. Discipline with regard to body language, tone of voice and the pace of delivery constitute extremely crucial considerations within the art and science of effective communications.

As a form of communication, the performance of classical music by a symphony orchestra serves as an excellent example with regard to sales presentations. The notes on a printed page do not constitute a concert. The notes only represent the script. Although important, the conductor (or sales director) only coordinates the content, timing and direction of performances. At the end of the day, only the audience or clients can ultimately judge the effectiveness of a presentation.

Although everyone uses the five senses of sight, sound, smell, touch and taste to determine personal orientation in the world, only two actually apply to the delivery of sales presentations – visual and auditory communication. The other senses remain pertinent on a certain level, but can always be described verbally and/or visually with words and pictures.

Every person processes millions of messages every second. Most of these messages are interpreted on a subconscious level. People then filter these messages through previous life experiences – the blueprint of their existence. Ultimately, a combination of these messages reaches the conscious mind, and people become aware of thoughts and ideas. However, people do not make decisions or take action based exclusively upon conscious rational thought. People quite often make decisions and take action based upon feelings that may not be so readily identifiable.

People frequently take action based upon gut feelings, and then think to themselves, "I don't know why I feel this way, but I do." People essentially react to sets of circumstances including facts and figures, but then take instinctive actions. Those instinctive actions are rarely entirely based on pure logic.

Throughout every sales presentation, clients internalize and react both consciously and subconsciously to only two types of stimuli, visual and audible communication. Knowledgeable application of specialized techniques relating to both types of message delivery systems is integral to the success of every sales communication endeavor. God gave you two ears and one mouth for a reason.

Visual Communications

Sales Environment and Collateral Material

Regardless of whether or not they realize it, clients take notice of every little thing during the course of a sales presentation. The physical environment associated with every sales presentation plays a vitally important role in the overall communications process. This includes the common areas of a sales center, the sales cubicles both individually and collectively and the automobiles used for transporting clients to the resort, as well as the resort property itself. All of these components should exemplify cleanliness and communicate a sense of orderliness and professionalism.

The physical environment around every sales presentation must also convey a sense of pride, integrity and credibility. Use souvenirs from personal travel, gifts from clients and other travel related paraphernalia to demonstrate passion for travel on a personal basis. Showcase plaques, framed certificates and other objects to demonstrate individual personality and levels of achievement. Visual aids such as photographs, charts, graphs, rendition drawings and other supportive collateral material impact clients in significant fashion. These materials should always be organized, and appear to be in mint condition. You should always have the latest, greatest, and the most up-to-date collateral material!

Physiology and Eye Contact

Clients also make conscious and subconscious judgments based upon the appearance of sales representatives. Body language plays an important role in every sales presentation ranging from stature and gestures to facial expressions and eye contact. These physiological factors serve to communicate personal commitment and internal comfort with the product offering without so much as a word being spoken. Facial expressions such as smiling, laughing and surprise convey a personal level of excitement and passion toward your clients and the product. Direct eye contact is essential to the conveyance of trust. It is critical to have the ability to respond to direct point blank questions by looking clients square in the eyes, and answering without blinking or looking away.

Audible Communications

Remember, passion can only be found in the delivery of a message. It's not what you say, but how you say it. Your pace, volume and tone of voice in every sales presentation must be varied and congruent with the messages being delivered. There is intrinsic value in matching and mirroring the mannerisms of clients both physically and verbally. This creates a commonality bond by causing your clients to subconsciously think that you are very much like them in many respects. If your clients speak quickly, then speak quickly. If your clients speak slowly, then speak slowly throughout the presentation.

Tone of Voice / Voice Inflections

Tone of voice is essential to bringing a calm sense of "Business as Usual" to your sales presentation. A proper tone of voice will trigger comfort within the minds of your clients, and cause them to think, "If everyone else is accepting timeshare as a better way of getting more out of their vacations, then we're going to do it too." Proper voice inflection keeps clients interested in what is being said throughout the course of your presentation. A monotone delivery becomes boring very quickly even if the information presented is inherently interesting.

Dynamics in the Delivery

Changing the volume of your voice, being dynamic - not monotone, during your presentation can also be used to express excitement or enthusiasm about the benefits of your product. This can be especially valuable when discussing undeniable truths or the Five Core Motivational Needs. Softly spoken words can be used to convey a sense of value and urgency, or for the purpose of sharing a secret. Changing the pace of delivery, voice inflections and volume within your presentation all serve the purpose of adding special emphasis to important thoughts and feelings, and can dramatically enhance your persuasiveness.

Syntax and Pace of Delivery

It is also important to use words and phrases that are easy to understand. Vocabulary and grammar play a large part in every sales presentation. Avoid terminology that only a person working within the timeshare industry would understand. It is equally important to pause from time to time throughout a presentation in order to give clients time to think. Pausing can create drama, and add emphasis to an important thought or feeling. Pausing even in mid-sentence can cause clients to anticipate what will be said next, and can serve to peak interest in a particular point. Pausing for a moment before giving an answer to a question will yield enhanced interest in the answer.

Communications Methodology

Lead-In Statements and Rhetorical Questions

The use of Lead-In Statements and Rhetorical Questions serve the dual purpose of maintaining control and providing reinforcement of fundamental concepts within a sales presentation. For example, if "Fear of Change" has been the subject matter of discussion, you might say, "So, if people want something different in their lives, they must _____ the way they have been doing it." Making clients fill in the blank or complete the statement keeps them participating in the presentation on an interactive basis, and actively thinking about the concept on a more personal basis.

Rhetorical Questions are questions where the answers will be consistent and obvious to everyone. They serve to emphasize and reinforce predictable perceptions and responses. For example, you might ask, "What must people do if they want something different in their lives?" Within the context of a discussion about the need for change, all clients will respond by saying, "Change." The goal is to cause participatory interaction with your clients in a controlled fashion.

Placement of Concepts and Ideas

The placement of an idea early in the presentation can also be a useful tool for causing clients to start thinking about accepting a concept or concern prior to its formal introduction. For example, you know you have a client touring for the first time and the concern will come up that they will need to do their research before buying. While talking about your developer's credibility, you might bring up the comment, "Many first time buyers like you tend to want to shop around prior to purchasing into an ownership program. I will share with you a little later how and why so many first timers understand the research that's already been done and chose to became owners with us."

Direct and Indirect Communication

Direct Communication involves the conveyance of information about the timeshare product, and the features and benefits of the product as related to the Five Core Motivational Needs. Indirect Communication involves the process of talking about general philosophical principles by discussing an idea or concept having no apparent connection to the timeshare product, and then later linking the principal or concept back to timeshare.

The Indirect Communication style is a little more difficult to comprehend than Direct Communication, but not difficult to implement once you are familiar with the technique. In theory, Indirect Communication is attempting to have your client think and say what you are persuading them to think and say. This is done by asking a question about your subject instead of making a direct statement. For example, instead of making the direct statement, "If you vacation more, you will become closer to your family and friends." You can ask the question, "What do you think happens to families that spend quality time together?"

Here is another example. Let's say your client is debating the Rent Versus Own logic of ownership. Instead of attacking the subject take the indirect approach and say, "When one becomes a vacation owner, they get wholesale pricing for life on their vacations. It's similar to buying your next soda in bulk instead of spending three times as much by buying them one can at a time."

Short stories or third party stories are great techniques for delivering both direct and indirect messages to clients. Some stories should directly relate to timeshare, and others should relate to important life principles with implications applicable to timeshare. The idea is to communicate valuable messages to clients without direct confrontation. Indirect stories serve as especially valuable tools when used to illustrate deep emotional decision making issues.

Teasers

The use of teasers can be very effective to hold the suspense of a key point or benefit. They are used so that your client continues to be interactive and held in suspense. An example might be, "When I start talking about how this works, I will share with you one of the most exciting features and benefits of vacation ownership." Or, "When we go to the property and we are standing in the model, remind me to point out one of the most impressive features and benefits of our resort."

Superlatives

The use of superlatives can be very powerful when you need to stress a key benefit or point. They make the point stand out as supreme, as the highest or most eminent focal point of what you are about to say. For example, if you are stressing the logic of ownership instead of renting vacations, make the statement, "If you don't get anything else out of my presentation, I want you to remember this! The most important reason that millions of people have become owners of their own vacations, and the reason millions of people join such programs today is because they are looking to get more value from the money they are going to spend anyway. They are looking to get more for less while maintaining a consistent high quality." Or, "The most important thing to remember about vacation ownership is the fact that most people will not justify spending the kind of money it takes to stay in the places you will experience with ownership."

Numbers

The use of numbers offers two distinctive benefits during the presentation. The first benefit of using numbers in your presentation is the list of benefits you are going to share becomes the focal point of your presentation. For example, "People to purchase into an ownership program are looking to achieve four distinctive benefits. First, consistent quality, second, something to show for their money, third, more value for the money they are going to spend anyway, and fourth, security knowing they can continue living the lifestyle of their choice." The second benefit comes into play when you intentionally omit the last benefit of your list. This becomes a test to gauge whether your client has been paying attention to your presentation. If they don't ask about the last benefit, you should internalize where you might have lost their interest so that you don't repeat misreading your clients.

Comparative Literary Devices

The following literary devices are extremely powerful ways to discuss your point of view or overcome a consumer's concerns without confrontation. Simply address your viewpoint or consumer concerns by discussing the issues as they relate to other topics, and then relate the conclusion of your point back to the timeshare concept.

Adage

An adage is a short saying, the wisdom of which has gained credit through long use.

Analogy

An analogy is the expression of similarity in some respects between things that are otherwise dissimilar, or a comparison based on such similarity. It is a form of logical inference, based on the assumption that if two things are known to be alike in some respects, they must be alike in other respects.

Anecdote

An anecdote is a short account of an interesting or humorous incident. Anecdotes contain secret or previously undisclosed details relating to either historical or biographical incidents.

Hypothetical Illustration

Hypothetical Illustration is the use of suppositional circumstances to draw conclusions as to appropriate action or conduct. It is a proposition stated as a basis for argument or reasoning, or a premise from which a conclusion can be drawn.

Metaphor

A metaphor is a figure of speech in which a word or phrase that ordinarily designates one thing is used to designate another, making an implicit comparison, as in "A sea of troubles" or "All the world is a stage." It is a figure of speech in which a term is transferred from the object it ordinarily designates to an object it may designate only by implicit comparison or analogy, as in the phrase "evening of life."

Newspaper Clippings, Periodicals and Current Affairs

Use newspaper clippings, magazine articles and a fundamental knowledge of current affairs to document or illustrate certain elements of your sales presentation.

Parable

Parables are simple stories used to illustrate a moral or religious lesson.

Simile

A simile is a figure of speech in which two essentially unlike things are compared, the comparison typically being made explicit with the use of the introductory words "like" or "as." For example, "Like ancient trees, we die from the top." "Timeshare is like a good bottle of wine. It gets better with age."

Quotations

Reference quotes from famous people to illustrate important points with clients.

Understatements

Understatements serve to express a concept with restraint or lack of emphasis, especially for dramatic impact.

Witty Humor

Use witty humor to engage clients both logically and emotionally. Humorous stories and quips serve to diffuse tension and relax clients. Obviously, ethnic jokes, sex, religion and politics should be avoided as subject matter. The most effective humor is an ad lib or spontaneous witty comeback to something that has been said in normal conversation. Remember this as the world's best kept secret. When they are laughing, they are buying. People cannot be in a happy brain and a sad or suspicious brain at the same time (as commonly viewed on the Discovery Channel). The alternative to the happy brain, or the happy place is the Lizard-Brain. Some other terms for the Lizard-Brain are:

Reptilian Brain

Old Brain

Lower Brain

The Brain Stem

The main function of the Lizard-Brain in all animals, including humans is fight, flight or freeze. When threatened, should I fight, should I try to escape or should I just stand perfectly still and hope no harm comes to me?

"When your clients are laughing they're buying.
Keep them away from the Lizard!"

~ Gecko

Chapter 13

THE LITMUS TEST

"A revealing test using a single indicator to prompt a *DECISION*."

The Litmus Test

What is a litmus test? In scientific terms, it is a piece of paper that will change color depending on whether a solution is more acidic or more alkaline. So how does this relate to selling? In sales, we have been taught to take clients' temperature as a measure of their preparedness to take positive action. It is like a Litmus Test. Just ask your clients trial closing questions during your presentation to find out if they are paying attention, and actively showing interest in moving forward. Asking Litmus Test Questions represents an invaluable technique and most salespeople know the value in doing them. So, the question arrives, "If we all know we must do this, then why don't more salespeople do it?"

Some of your clients' fears or Action Inhibitors have been addressed in this book. Would you agree these fears are real and valid when it comes to your clients? Okay, so if your clients have fears, would you say it is possible that salespeople may also have some fears?

You have probably heard of the 80/20 rule. Eighty percent of the sales force makes twenty percent of the money and twenty percent of the sales force makes eighty percent of the money. Here is a rhetorical question for you, "Which group do you want to be in?"

So why are so many salespeople just average? Because salespeople have their own fears, just like their clients. Salespeople have very normal fears, including the fear of rejection, the fear of failure and the fear of conflict. These fears are obstacles that keep salespeople from asking clients trial closing questions which are supposed to provide a guide to the direction of a sale. The top 20% of the sales force out there have overcome their own fears of rejection, and will ask every client to buy every time. The other 80% have some type of fear regarding rejection which prevents them from asking their clients to buy every time.

Now, we are not all afraid of rejection, failure and conflict, but then why do most salespeople remain part of the 80%? It is either because they know what to do, and just choose not to do it, or they just don't know what to do. They do not understand or they do not care! Is this you? Which group do you fit into? So, what does having fear cause? It causes salespeople to back off. It causes salespeople to hesitate when they should have the courage to proceed. When asking a trial closing question and a favorable response is not received, what happens? Internally, there is some level of tension that builds because now the salesperson feels the need to confront the objection. So instead of feeling this discomfort on a continuous basis, what do many salespeople do? Isn't this exactly what all people do? These salespeople move away from the questions which cause pain, and tend to seek the pleasure of assuming things are moving toward a sale.

The Litmus Test is a set time during the presentation where you will automatically ask your client if the information has been favorable so far. There have been many studies done regarding how many times during the sales process a client must be asked to buy. You must ask for the sale five, 10 or even 20 times during your presentations! An example would be, "Are you in yet?" or, "Do you want one yet?" or, "What's the one thing, the exact thing, that you need from me today in order to move forward?" or, "Can I welcome you as our newest owners?" Isolate, Isolate, Isolate!

When you have a set screen play designed to relate around a broad based market and it encompasses all the techniques, you should trial close throughout the presentation. However, strategically placing test questions within your presentation will help move your clients forward toward a purchase. There is a presentation study out which suggests that you must ask your buyer three times in a sequential order of increased directness to consider your product before the final purchasing decision is made. After every Litmus Test Question, continue to build more value around your product until the final request to purchase.

The sequential order is:

Non Timeshare Owner

- So far, are you thinking the concept of ownership is making sense for you? Why?
- Does the "x" program sound like it will work for you today?
- What you will need to do is fill out the top part of this worksheet.

Timeshare Owner

- So far, are you thinking that adding another week will greatly enhance your future vacation plans? Why?
- Are you definitely thinking of adding another week? Why?
- What you will need to do is fill out the top part of this worksheet.

Having the Litmus Test Questions in your presentation is powerful because it forces you to ask set questions in specific places giving you the insight as to where your clients are in the purchasing process. You will know if they are moving forward towards ownership, or know if you have more work to do. Remember, it is always *you* that needs to work harder and smarter!

"Time or Money?

Time is wisdom.

Money is youthful enthusiasm."

~ Enlightenment

"Those who believe and conceive will achieve a career."

~ Master Closer

"Success is never final, failure is never fatal.

It's courage that counts."

~ John Wooden

PART II

"THE WHY"

12 STEPS TO SUCCESS

PRESENTATION

"THE WHY"

12 STEPS TO SUCCESS

1) MEET AND GREET

2) WALL TOUR

3) CLIENT PROFILE

4) RECAP

5) INTENT TO SELL

6) WHY TODAY / CLUB CERT

7) WHY VACATION

8) EXCHANGE

9) WHY TIMESHARE / RENT vs. OWN

10) PRODUCT

11) PROPERTY/MODEL TOUR

12) CLOSE

"THE WHY"

12 STEPS TO SUCCESS

1. <u>MEET AND GREET</u> (Create Fun)

   1) Non-Verbal Communication
   2) Verbal Communication
   3) Social Questions

2. <u>WALL TOUR</u> (Build Excitement)

   1) Company Credibility

3. <u>CLIENT PROFILE</u> (Listen and Gather…No Selling Yet)

   1) Clients' Personal Information
   2) Past, Present, Future

4. <u>RECAP</u> (Show How Much You Care)

   1) Associate Info to the Five Core Motivational Needs
   2) What Matters Most
   3) Confirm the Emotional Reason
   4) Clarify their wants and needs
   5) Earn their trust by repeating back
   6) Forward-moving Statement

5. <u>INTENT TO SELL</u> (Amp it Up; Use Passion and Conviction)

    1) Time Acknowledgement
    2) Need Statement
    3) Take-a-way
    4) Greed Statement
    5) Urgency Statement
    6) Action Statement
    7) Manager Support
    8) Permission to Sell

6. <u>WHY TODAY / CLUB CERT</u> (The Law of the Sale)

    1) First Day / Initial Visit Incentives
    2) Compliance Trial Closes

7. <u>WHY VACATION</u> (Solve Their Problems with Vacations)

    1) The Purpose of Life
    2) It's All About Relationships
    3) Routine vs. Quality Time
    4) The Vacation Commitment
    5) Story Time

8. <u>EXCHANGE</u> (Getaways and Vacation Commitment)

    1) Justify the Value
    2) How the System Works
    3) Quality of the Network
    4) Time Out

9. <u>WHY TIMESHARE / RENT VS. OWN</u> (14.9% vs. 100% LO$$)

    1) Why Timeshare
    2) Consumer Concerns
    3) Timeshare Sense
    4) Financial Breakdown
    5) Financial Logic / Rent vs. Own

10. <u>PRODUCT</u> (Product Recommendation and Worksheet)

    1) Explain the Product (Keep it Simple)
    2) Fill out the Worksheet 100%

11. <u>PROPERTY/MODEL TOUR</u> (Commitment Trial Closes)

    1) Overview
    2) Site Tour (Sizzle)
    3) Property Services
    4) Residence
    5) Sell the Experience

12. <u>CLOSE</u> (Welcome Your Newest Owners!)

    1) Recap the emotional reasons your clients will buy this today
    2) Recap the problems that were solved with Vacation Ownership
    3) Remind your clients of the benefits and also the fear of loss
    4) Get buy-in agreement from all parties
    5) Be happy, transfer positive energy, close the deal and get the sale

Success

Do you want to be outstanding? Do you want to be extraordinary? Success doesn't happen overnight. Becoming great in the timeshare business requires aggressive commitment. It takes discipline to always learn and grow because the timeshare industry and human behavior consistently change. Your success will be directly related to the amount of time and effort you dedicate to studying and learning the sales process. Selling timeshare is a procedure, a series of steps that build upon one another to the final outcome of a sale. Although it requires a lot of training and hard work, remember that selling timeshare, and changing people's lives for the better, is a lot of fun.

The steps of the selling process you are learning from this book have been designed with the help of some of the most successful salespeople in the timeshare industry. The material and insight has come from many ARDA Award Winners which represents the best of the best as determined by the American Resort Development Association. When studied daily and applied daily, you too will become one of the great names in the industry.

Having a specific structure is critical because it will serve as your road map to success. If you needed to drive from Point A to Point B and needed directions, a map would show the way to your final destination. In selling, the structure is your map, and the destination is having consumers feel you have just improved their lives. Once memorized and understood, it will no longer be necessary to think about what to do next, or what to say next. Instead, you will be able to totally focus intently upon what your clients are saying and doing during the course of your presentation. The structure also lets you know when your clients are leading the presentation in the wrong direction so that you can steer them back, and continue to the destination where you need to be going. You must always remember to keep the end result in mind at all times, and follow the course to a sale. Understanding "THE WHY" of the 12 Steps to Success will bring continuous successful selling and closing.

Within the structure of your presentation, there are five independent external focuses to understand. These five items encompass all sales transactions. When you take the time to master each one, and then set goals with direction to improve your understanding of how they impact your ability to sell, you will become truly disciplined and tremendously successful.

1. Salesperson: You must understand who you are, and what role you play within the company. You are not a customer service representative. You should not care about, nor allow yourself to be sidetracked by, the company's internal political environment. Do not concern yourself with anything other than information that will help you accomplish the goal of your chosen career, and that is to make sales. The only thing that matters is your ability to persuade clients to make a purchase. All of your actions, behavior, and focus should always be oriented toward the end result because, at the end of the day, you will not get paid for anything other than selling the product.

2. Communication: You should communicate in a simple, yet effective manner. Remain cognizant of your verbiage, tone, pace, inflection and expression. Are you really listening to what your clients are saying?

3. Physiology: Is your body language matching your focus and fundamental belief in what you are selling?

4. Conviction: Are you a person of integrity sharing the pros and cons of what you are selling? Have you turned your passion into personal belief? Do you maintain a positive mental state of mind?

   Trust and integrity come from you and the company. Clients must know that the company you represent is dependable, and that they will receive support after the sale. You must portray your company as having a good reputation, and that it will deliver whatever you promise.

Does the product and services you represent fulfill a genuine need? Will it solve an existing or future problem for your clients? This addresses their hidden agenda. They will always be asking themselves "What's in it for me?"

Buyers want value for their investments. Your clients must be convinced that your product or service has value to them. If they feel otherwise, no price will ever be right. Don't push price, sell intrinsic value. If clients are convinced they are getting real value, they will be less resistant to price considerations. When consumers have a compelling need or desire for a product, price becomes much less important.

5. Timing: Professional selling is a transferable skill. You must know when to ask for the order as well as how to ask for the order. When the other four purchasing criteria have been met in positive fashion, the only logical decision left is when to buy.

When selling becomes a procedure, it ceases to be a problem. Conversely, if it is not a procedure, selling successfully will always be a problem. Within the pages that follow, you will learn the structure for success. It is now up to you, and how you use the information that will ultimately determine the outcome. As the Darwinian Theory states, "We are all changing. Either we are evolving and growing, or we are dying and being replaced." There is no neutral zone here. Are you changing and growing, or will you be left behind?

Compare the foundation of a house with the foundation of the sales process as it relates to structural integrity. When building a house, it is critical to first create a good foundation. It is impossible to build a house without a solid foundation. Without a proper foundation, the house will be faulty and not level. The structure could fall, or crack in half. The same concept applies to the sales process.

In the sales process, the foundation is crucial. Without it, you can never have a beginning. The corner stone of the foundation in every sales presentation is the creation of trust and credibility. If your clients don't have a sense that you care about them and their needs as people, will they listen to what you have to say? If they don't respect your knowledge of the product and associated services, or believe in your company's reputation to deliver what is promised, will they accept your message to change the way they vacation?

As the old adage goes, "People don't care how much you know until they know how much you care." Create a connection with your clients, and establish a setting where they feel comfortable and relaxed. Only then will they be open minded enough to listen. Establishing a good foundation for the presentation involves setting the pace and tone of the meeting. Do not come across as a salesperson. Be a vacation counselor or vacation consultant instead. Show personality through personal actions and behavior. Show a caring demeanor, and demonstrate a desire to help others. Establish early on that the meeting is for the benefit of your clients, and that it is a business relationship.

Without a doubt, the tendency to prejudge clients when greeting them is one of the toughest hurdles to get past. Just like the saying, "You can never judge a book by its cover," prejudging clients by what they put on a profile sheet, or by how they dress and look, is insane. How often do clients come into a presentation actually looking to make a purchase? They want to get out, so what kind of information will they initially provide? Prejudging is one of the most difficult things to suppress because it is human nature to prejudge. However, it is critical to deliver a powerful presentation each and every time regardless of your clients' appearance or what they say.

So what does it take to perform a powerful presentation? Preparation! "You reap what you sow" has no short cuts. Success builds on success and becoming truly successful in this industry not only requires mastering the techniques and principles of the presentation but mastering your internal attitude and conviction. Before diving into the modules of the presentation, here are some helpful thoughts to consider.

One's belief will ultimately determine ones outcome. Belief is self-fulfilling, because if you believe something is possible or believe it isn't, you're right either way. Your belief in who you are and what you sell is invaluable and the greater it is, the more powerful your message will be. In order to strengthen your presentation, you need to gain a pure conviction regarding this industry, your developer, the area where your resort is located, the programs offered, and most importantly, the intangible benefits that vacations offer people.

The following steps will help you gain confidence in your knowledge of the industry, and therefore becoming more charismatic.

1. Learn about the growth and history of the timeshare industry.

    ✓ Review the Arda.org website regularly
    ✓ Read Developments Magazine
    ✓ Read Vacation World Magazine

2. Talk with owners at your resort.
3. Take vacations.
4. Visit other developments in your area to create comparative value.
5. Talk with other industry professionals to get their feedback on the industry.
6. Put together photo albums of personal vacations.
7. Visit or stay at timeshare resorts when you vacation.
8. Encourage your team/management to have sales contests, and then stay at Premiere/Gold Crown resorts.

Walk the Talk

Once you have the confidence and you are expressing it with conviction, performance comes with continued focus. If you continue to give your time and energy, results happen. If someone wanted to be a professional golfer, will they achieve it by having positive thinking only? No, they would need to consistently practice hitting thousands of golf balls before they might gain the consistency necessary for greatness. There are one hit wonders that have pulled out a miracle win on occasion, but the true champions are the ones that consistently perform day in and day out. When the opportunity arises, they were the ones called upon to bring the team to victory. Rarely do consumers come determined to purchase and when they do, anyone can make the sale. The best salespeople practice and focus on success daily for consistent performance. They are the ones called in when the team needs to pull out their numbers.

Mental Imagery

What your mind can believe and conceive, it will achieve. Visualizing success is a powerful technique used by most successful individuals. When the mind's eye visualizes an experience or action with given results, it will imprint the experience to memory. Then, when it comes time to go live, the situation and surroundings are familiar. The pressure, anxiety and nervousness is diminished greatly. Asking for or achieving something one has not experienced yet brings with it a certain level of emotional satisfaction.

If you wanted to start selling packages beyond your comfort level, how would you go about it? Let's say you want to sell two week packages. The first step is you must believe you can. The next step would be to visualize asking a client to buy a two week package. The third step would be to actually start asking clients to purchase two weeks, and show value as to why they should do so. If you followed this sequence, at some point do you believe you will achieve your goal? Mental imagery's strength and power comes from placing yourself into the mental picture and visualizing the outcome desired. Take the time to practice visualizing the sale before meeting your clients. Visualize your clients as your newest owners. Once you have mastered this technique you will always smile brighter and appear much happier. The effect of visualization is contagious and your clients will feel your positive energy. All that you believe and conceive you will achieve through this transference of optimistic, affirmative and constructive energy. Remember, the only thing in life that you can truly control is your attitude… *attitude is altitude.*

"I can't coach the uncoachable.
I can't coach the stubborn!
Are you coachable and willing to change?"

~ Coach Proccacini

Chapter 14

THE FOUR BASICS

"Always keep the end result in mind."

THE FOUR BASICS

Basic 1   **FRONT-END BUMP**
End of CLIENT PROFILE

Basic 2   **CONFERENCE**
Prior to PRODUCT

Basic 3   **WORKSHEET**
End of PRODUCT

Basic 4   **T.O. (Management Closing Assistance)**
At the CLOSE, turn the table with a positive and exciting RECAP. Clear your desktop of all mess/junk that might accumulate during sales presentations. The only items on your desk should be:

1. Client Profile Survey Sheet

2. Worksheet (100% completely filled out)

3. Club Certificate

4. Rent vs. Own Sheet

5. Vacation Exchange Directory

THE FOUR BASICS represent a parallel technique to be overlaid onto the 12 STEPS TO SUCCESS in order to encourage engagement between you and your tour guests, and your Sales Manager as a friend. This process is designed to make your clients feel like valued guests in your home. They are interspersed within the 12 STEPS TO SUCCESS as follows:

THE FOUR BASICS

Basic 1   Front-End Bump – End of CLIENT PROFILE

The Front-End Bump allows you to nonchalantly introduce your manager to your clients as your friend. "I'd like to introduce you to my friend, David." By doing this, your clients are not approached by someone they don't know when you call your manager for assistance later in your presentation. It also gives your manager an opportunity to meet your clients and to get a better feel for their interest in the presentation and their interest in the idea of ownership. Introducing your manager as your friend is much less intimidating than if you introduced your manager at the end of your presentation, which may have your clients thinking or saying, "Oh, so this must be the Closer," or, "Who are you, the Closer?" This friendship step alleviates and prevents what could very easily be a very uncomfortable event in your presentation. Your Sales Manager will thank you for implementing this simple, but extremely important step. It is always better to experience kindness from all parties involved in the sale including your clients, who are valued guests in your home, your manager, yourself, and whoever else might be part of your sales presentation.

Basic 2   Conference – Prior to PRODUCT

The Conference is a great opportunity to run your ideas by your Sales Manager in order to get some feedback, and possibly some valuable redirection prior to your product recommendation. Before you explain to your clients how their specific ownership would work, step away for a few moments, give your clients a task to do in your absence, and find your manager to discuss your ideas. If you feel that you need to change your product recommendation, you can seek out additional guidance from your manager. This method of increased, more frequent communication with management is essential so that all parties involved are presenting the same ideas to your clients. Remember, change is guaranteed in every sales presentation, and this is where change happens. You must present change to your clients because it is essential to get the deal. The purpose of the conference is to reveal to your manager what you truly believe your clients will spend today on your product. You can also get expert advice as to innovative ways to overcome objections.

Basic 3   Worksheet – End of PRODUCT

After you have made your product recommendation, but before the Property/Model Tour, fill out a worksheet completely with your clients. You should attempt to gain agreement as you say aloud the things you are writing such as, "You remember the 14.9% interest rate? And remember, there is no prepayment penalty on that." When you call for a manager's assistance it is critical that all pricing, dates, inventory and financing is filled out on the worksheet. Your manager is going to be closing from the worksheet to help overcome the "today" issue. The worksheet should be filled out completely. Every space should be completed. Don't be lazy. Avoid shortcuts. Isolate on the down payment and the monthly payment. This is the time to ask if both are comfortably affordable. If not, you should have another conference with your manager for further guidance and assistance. This requires more work. However, it is essential that your clients can afford what you are showing them. If they cannot afford what you have laid out on the worksheet, you must recommend a change before showing the property. For example, you can say, "Let's take a look at the property. I will ask my manager to see if he can do something extremely special to help make this a great fit for your family." The sale has just begun, and you must persevere through this very exciting challenge. Remember, in sales you get an "A" for selling. What do you think you get for not selling?

Basic 4   T.O. (Management Closing Assistance)

When you call your friend/manager back to your table for help finding special inventory, you should turn the table with a positive RECAP, or TURN. This overview should reiterate all of the emotional reasons why your clients will probably buy your product today. If you created a true problem and solved it with timeshare, you are proceeding toward a sale. Your recap should also highlight what they really loved about the ownership or property and why it is so important to them to own today. You should always link their emotional motivator to your First Day Incentives. Linking what they want more of in their lives to your property/timeshare will definitely increase your "today" closing percentage. Your manager will be extremely pleased with this type of TURN.

One last reminder, "Silence is golden," and "He who speaks first loses" when your clients are asked the definitive closing question. As an agent, you should never, ever speak once you have turned over your clients to your manager. (This is what T.O. stands for - your manager Takes Over.) Practice this skill because it is one of the most challenging steps that you can learn to master. When the student is ready, the master will appear. Someday you will be a manager, and you will realize how important this process is to your bottom line.

To Close: To join, unite, shut complete, to bring together all of the elements to end and finish. To surround and advance upon, so as to eliminate the possibility of escape. Not easily to acquire, scarce, as credit or money. Bound by mutual interest, loyalties or affections. The art of closing; conclusion, finish. Proximate in time, space and relationship, all encompassing.

"Did you close them, or did they close themselves?"

~ Grasshopper

On the next page, THE FOUR BASICS are shown overlaid onto the 12 STEPS TO SUCCESS for you to review and study. (THE FOUR BASICS are *italicized*.)

"THE WHY"

12 STEPS TO SUCCESS with THE FOUR BASICS

1) MEET AND GREET

2) WALL TOUR

3) CLIENT PROFILE

Basic 1   *Front-End Bump (end of CLIENT PROFILE)*

4) RECAP

5) INTENT TO SELL

6) WHY TODAY / CLUB CERT

7) WHY VACATION

8) EXCHANGE

9) WHY TIMESHARE / RENT VS. OWN

Basic 2   *Conference (Prior to PRODUCT)*

10) PRODUCT

Basic 3   *Worksheet (End of PRODUCT)*

11) PROPERTY/MODEL TOUR

12) CLOSE

Basic 4   *T. O. (Management Closing Assistance)*

(Turn the table with a positive and exciting RECAP)

Chapter 15

1. MEET AND GREET

"*I AM FUN*. I love people and people love me."

"*I AM FUN*"

<u>MEET AND GREET</u> – Create Fun

Clients start making instantaneous assessments and judgments about you immediately upon your initial meeting and greeting. They evaluate everything from the way you walk to the way you initially communicate with them. The initial greeting should be designed to gain rapport with your clients. It is not a matter of becoming best friends with them within five minutes, but rather convincing them that you have their best interests in mind. Your client should also get a sense of trust and credibility that you know and understand people's needs, and they should get a sense that you are paying attention to what they have to say. Only then will they feel compelled to pay attention to what you have to say.

The very best salespeople have the ability to establish rapport quickly, and build connections with clients that let their clients know that they care about them. Clients must feel certain that you care about their personal needs, desires and values. Clients must know that you share a vital interest in whatever is most important to them and their families.

Every opportunity for personal interaction with clients includes the communication of a myriad of non-verbal messages. Most of these messages are innate to the essential nature of people, and as a result, can be very difficult to manipulate and control. However, there are several key techniques that can be very helpful in establishing a good first impression. Remember, you have only one opportunity to make a good first impression.

Establishing a connection with your clients is broken down into three categories. The first category deals with your physiology, the way you carry yourself. This is Non-Verbal Communication. The next category deals with the style you use to start communicating with your clients. This is Verbal Communication. Finally, the last category is the specific dialogue you use to begin your relationship with your clients, or Personal Information.

Non-Verbal Communication

There are a myriad of non-verbal messages communicated by every interaction between people. These messages are subconscious and ingrained in your personality and how you carry yourself. Changing your non-verbal messages can be extremely difficult because they make up the essence of your personality, but knowing some of the following key techniques can help you establish a good first impression.

1. **Body Posture:** Does your posture emit confidence, credibility, excitement and sincerity? Remember, there is a direct correlation between body posture and how people internally view themselves and others. Without being pretentious, make sure that clients recognize the personal and professional success you have already achieved.

2. **Smile:** Show a soft, warm, sincere and friendly smile. Be sure to smile because everyone's natural reaction will be to smile back.

3. **Eye Contact:** Make sure to acknowledge both husband and wife by making direct eye contact with each. Acknowledge their kids and offer a sincere compliment. Making eye contact conveys a sense of trust and expresses a sense of caring. Use the technique of "kind eyes" by thinking wonderful thoughts about your clients – it shows because are your eyes are smiling. It is very important to have "Smiling Eyes."

4. **Hand Shake:** Extend your hand to your client and mimic their handshake. A reasonably firm handshake will communicate strength and confidence, but don't be overbearing with your grip.

5. **Match and Mirror:** Experts report that only seven percent of communication comes from the words stated. The remaining is how you say the spoken words and your physiology. Matching and Mirroring is a very advanced technique that takes a commitment to learn and master. It is called NeuroLinguistic Programming. Many excellent books have been written on this subject. Using this technique will cause your clients to feel comfortable and at ease.

6. **Gestures:** Hand gestures and other physiological methods of communication should match those of your clients as much as humanly possible. Pay attention to their reaction to your movements in order to ascertain whether or not those actions are causing a distraction.

Verbal Communication

Verbal communication is the transition from the initial prejudging image being created to establishing a connection with your clients by sharing information about yourself.

1. **First Names:** Get to know your clients on a first name basis right away. Whether repeating their names mentally to commit them to memory, or outwardly stating them, repetition will help you remember their names. The more you repeat, the more you retain so use your clients names. Clients love to hear their names!

2. **Find Commonality:** When you are trying to find commonality, the mind cannot tell the difference between the past, present or future. Commonality can be similar interests, family upbringing, geographical relations, educational interests or social values. Commonality works both ways. If you find a connection with your client, and you begin to like them, do you think you might have a better chance of making a sale? Sales people sell people they like. Conversely, consumers buy from people they like. Commonality is getting a sense of a "me too" relationship. When you have a profile sheet, pay attention to the information, and use it for this purpose. Another technique to finding commonality is to pay attention to the words your clients use, and then incorporating them into your presentation.

3. **Give a sincere Compliment:** People have an innate desire to be appreciated and acknowledged. Try to find something you genuinely like about your clients, and share it with them within the first few minutes of your initial greeting. It's difficult not to like someone who is being nice to you. Find something about them that you have in common, and compliment them on that

interest. Always attempt to find something you love about your newest owners.

4. **Social Questions:** Initial conversation should include a natural series of questions designed to get to know your clients on a personal basis. They should not be directed towards business, but rather relate to general basic factual information. Ask your clients where they live, how many children they have in their family and how they have enjoyed their vacation so far.

> "Where do you folks live?"
> "Do you have children?"
> "Are you having a good time in town?"
> "What has been the best part of your vacation so far?"
> "What are you doing for fun while you are here?"

During the initial greeting, your clients will be measuring you up just as much as you are measuring them up. These techniques will help you establish quick rapport, and have your clients start connecting with you. The idea here is to make them feel the need to pay attention, listen and actively participate in your presentation.

During this time, it's very important to take notice to see if your clients are becoming engaged in the presentation and paying attention to you. Some of the warning signs to look for are:

> Are they looking around when you are speaking with them?
> When someone walks by, do they turn their heads and look?
> Are their arms crossed or are they looking downward?

When this is happening, take notice and take action. Do not let this behavior persist because the bottom line is no active participation equals no sale.

This behavior is common to clients with no interest. Your goal is to convince them that the time dedicated to your presentation will be worth their while, and that the information presented will be both interesting and valuable.

Personal Information

Keep this short, sweet and on target. The establishment of friendship normally takes a period of several years. People trust their friends with personal information, and naturally seek advice from the friends they trust the most. Friendship starts with the dissemination of personal information, and with enough common ground, a level of trust is built. It is impossible to establish a lifelong friendship in 90 minutes, but it is possible to create a personal connection with your clients in expeditious fashion. Your clients must believe that you have a fundamental understanding of their needs in life, and that you care about them on a personal basis.

In order to make friends and gain trust with clients, it is necessary to establish credibility. Explain personal and professional accomplishments in life with the objective of giving clients a reason to listen and participate in the presentation. Describe the level of success achieved by the development company, and use that success as an explanation for having chosen to be associated with that company. Mention hobbies and personal interests as they relate to your clients, and be personable so that they have the feeling that they can interrupt and ask questions without causing offense.

Within the sales process, the use of personal information is not to create the depth of trust in social life, but to create a connection with your client. The focus is for you to share personal things about yourself so they feel comfortable reciprocating. You want to convey the perception that whether or not they decide to do business with the company you represent, the time spent will be worth their while. There are five items to focus on:

1) **Credibility:** Present credentials such as educational background and personal accomplishments. Clients need to believe in you before they will take the time to listen to what you are saying. Why would they listen to someone for whom they have no respect?

2) **Success in the industry:** Share personal reasons for joining this particular company as opposed to all of the other timeshare resorts in the world.

3) **Hobbies or Activities:** Discuss personal interests, and match the interests of your clients whenever possible. Describe your personal attraction to the resort area or town in which your property is located and describe some of the local activities that may be of mutual interest.

4) **Be Yourself:** Sharing personal information helps create a common bond with clients. People start relating to each other when they know a little bit about the person with whom they are dealing. Try to show your clients that you are human just like them. It is important to come across as a real person trying to accomplish the same things in life that your clients are trying to accomplish. Most importantly, downplay the importance of getting a sale for your personal needs.

5) **Your Mission Statement:** We do not remember days. We remember moments in our lives. The motto, "Always Great Vacations" should be the underlying theme of your presentations.

Order of the Day (Agenda)

The Order of The Day is a very basic and simple statement of the flow associated with your presentation. Your clients will get a feeling as to how the presentation is going to progress, and how it is going to make them feel. When people become familiar with their surroundings, they become more comfortable and relaxed. During the Order of the Day, keep it light and factual. The Order of the Day should contain the following elements:

- Sales Center Facilities
- Personal Office Space
- Transportation Requirements
- Timeframe of Presentation

DO NOT address any objections that may arise during this step.

Lightly put aside any buying concerns or time issues your clients may express as No Big Deal. The focus of this step is to continue building the foundation of trust and credibility, setting the stage for delivering a great presentation where your clients will be involved and participating. However, if your clients tell you they have an appointment or activity scheduled for after the tour, you must be considerate of their time and not go too long. You don't want your clients to time-close you!

"In everyone's life, at some time, the inner fire goes out. It is then burst into flame by an encounter with another human being. We should all be thankful for those people who rekindle the inner spirit."

~ Albert Schweitzer

"To Inspire is to Live In Spirit."

~ Guardian Angel

Chapter 16

2. WALL TOUR

"I AM thriving on *HIGH ENERGY!"*

"I AM HIGH ENERGY"

<u>WALL TOUR</u> – Build Excitement

Company Credibility

When thinking of credibility, there are two important components that come to mind. The first one has to do with you. Do you exhibit actions and motives in the right place? Do you exude the traits associated with a person of integrity and sound principles? Do you genuinely care about people, and helping people achieve their goals? Consumers buy their salesperson (you) as much as they buy the product.

Company Credibility is established within the first steps of the presentation because familiarity builds confidence and trust. It is the same reason you share personal information with your clients. You want your clients to feel comfortable with you and your company. They need this level of comfort with both you and your company before they will even consider doing business.

In today's market, consumers have more choices than ever as to where they can spend their money. Go to the grocery store, and look at how many different kinds of cereal are available! Stores dedicate entire aisles to cereal because of the number of choices today. How about cars? In 1907, Ford Motor Company produced only one type of automobile, the Model T. Now, there are hundreds of models from which to choose. Because consumers are bombarded with so many choices, it is important to acknowledge that your company is not the only one with which they could choose to do business. However, based on the credibility of your company and its product, it is one of the "Best of the Best" in the timeshare industry.

It is also important during your WALL TOUR to understand any concerns your clients might have regarding a purchase. First time buyers are normally thinking about doing research so that they can make an informed decision. Help them with the research they want to do while they are on tour. Otherwise, they will want to do it later! Owners of timeshare might be wondering why they should buy from you and your company rather than acquiring more time at their own resort. Emphasize the strengths of your company to alleviate these concerns.

When presenting your company and its product, highlight all the qualities inherent to both. The following is a list of benefits to consider:

- Geographical Strengths
- Product Design and Amenities
- Local, National and International Awards
- Expertise of Service Departments
- Commitment to Community
- Cultural Ethics and Integrity
- Discipline and Commitment to Customer Service
- Success of the Organization, Number of Owners, Years in Business

When consumers are confident that your product can meet their needs and expectations, the natural tendency is for them to assess whether or not the product can improve or enhance their lives. Credibility is all about trust. It is critical to convey a solid sense of trust. If your clients choose to do business with your company, they need to feel assured that your company is trustworthy, and that it will be consistently dedicated to delivering the experience they expect of your product.

The WALL TOUR should be infused with excitement and fun. You should be informative and high energy, moving quickly and purposefully through all your bullet points. The reason you will always be enthusiastic is that you are transferring your energy and momentum to your clients. Your performance is changing their emotional state from apathetic to appreciative. The WALL TOUR will take seven to ten minutes of time. However, it will feel like one minute to your clients because of your extreme, powerful presentation. Remember, great actors always get paid more than teachers. Therefore, go for the standing ovation every single time you do a WALL TOUR.

"Exciting, Exhilarating and Enthusiastic"

~ M.C. Energy

Chapter 17

3. CLIENT PROFILE

"*I AM* terrific at *LISTENING*!"

"*I AM LISTENING*"

<u>CLIENT PROFILE</u> – Listen and Gather (no selling yet!)

The CLIENT PROFILE will be totally about your clients. Your main purpose is to gather information so that you can link the features and benefits of your resort or program back to your clients' personalized Emotional Motivators later in your presentation. The biggest mistake salespeople make is selling too early, usually right after the initial MEET AND GREET. So that you do not totally destroy trust, you must wait to sell and close until it is appropriate - after the INTENT TO SELL statement. Whether you are new to the business or a seasoned professional, never sell while discovering what is important to your clients during this step of your presentation. You must be listening and gathering information from your clients to understand what is most important to them. When gathering this information, you must recognize which of their emotional reasons will cause them to take an Action Step toward purchasing today. Find out what they want more of in their lives, and then later, show them how timeshare can give them more of what they want and need.

There is much value in truly getting to know your clients and what motivates them. If it were possible to find out your clients' innermost values and then link them back to vacation ownership each and every time, virtually every client would purchase. But how often do your clients typically say, "Yes?" How often are they understood to this level? Being familiar with the Five Core Motivational Needs allows you to find out which of these needs is the highest priority for your clients and the specifics surrounding what is most important to them. This information is your clients' Emotional Motivator, or the reason that they will want to purchase from you today. Remember the Five Core Motivational Needs are Health, Safety, Love, Financial Security and Better Quality of Life.

Profiling your clients is also about learning what they have done for vacations in the past, how they are currently traveling and explore what kind of vacationing they would like to do in the future. Also, find out if there are any events or circumstances in their lives, real or imagined, that might prevent them from making a purchase today.

During this fact gathering step, there are two potential road blocks that may need to be handled. Depending on your clients' level of comfort with you and the format of the presentation, they might be resistant to participating because they are still looking for a way out as soon as possible. These road blocks are:

No Travel Commitment:

If your clients are suspicious of your intentions, or for unknown reasons have a dislike of timeshare, they might try to give a sense that they don't like to travel or that they have no desire to travel. This doesn't necessarily mean a sale is not possible. It is difficult to assess if your clients are being honest in their responses. They may not have consciously linked any of the Five Core Motivational Needs to the benefits of travel. They may not have connected the dots regarding the benefits of health, romance, adventure or improved relationships with friends or family as these things relate to travel. If a commitment to travel cannot be detected, it is imperative to share the value and benefits related to a life filled with new experiences.

General Objections:

Your clients may try to redirect the presentation by saying things like, "I would never do anything today." They might say "I think timeshare doesn't make sense," or, "We don't travel this way. We camp or stay with family and friends." This is not the time to deal with Consumer Concerns or objections. Have patience, but maintain control. Follow the established presentation format, not one of your clients' making. There is a time and place to address these issues, and you may find the concerns brought up now are not real or not important later on. Continue asking questions, but remember their real concerns so that you can bring them up when you can either overcome them or show that they are not really a reason not to buy.

When profiling clients, it is important to differentiate between the Timeshare Owners and Non-Timeshare Owners. Have specific questions for Timeshare Owners, and others for Non-Timeshare Owners. Gather the information in a conversational way. Do not make your CLIENT PROFILE an interrogation!

Non-Timeshare Owners

Your questions should yield a sense of your clients' spending habits and travel patterns. This is extremely important because it is a waste of time to discuss a product that is out of their price range. Many times, they will state at the very end that if they were going to buy, they would buy the best program. However, they will say that right now it is not affordable, and as a result, they are not going to purchase. They'll say the timing is not right. The objective of profiling your clients is to get a picture of the type of traveling they have done in the past, and a realistic sense of what they might like to do in the future so that you can determine what they will spend today.

Past: Questions regarding past travel patterns should be designed to gather information about how much money your clients have spent on travel over the years, where they have traveled and what type of accommodations they normally choose. Also, ask questions relating to past timeshare presentations they may have attended in order to find out why they did not purchase those.

Present: These questions should be designed to get information about what your clients are currently doing in the way of travel. Are there circumstances in their lives that may prevent them from traveling? Has travel fallen out of favor with them? Are career responsibilities or something else affecting their ability or desire to travel? How often do they travel, and how much money do they spend for their current traveling?

Future: These questions need to elicit favorable emotional responses by getting your clients to dream about the future. Get them to start thinking, contemplating, and discovering problems that need to be addressed in order for them to have quality vacations in the future. Purchasing timeshare is done in the moment, the today sale. Timeshare is sold for the future as a hope for a better, happier and more compelling life.

Timeshare owners

Your questions should be designed to lead your clients into the future. After assessing what they own, how they acquired it, if they are using it, and how they like it, ask if their existing ownership has accomplished what they initially purchased it to do. If there were anything they would change about their existing ownership, what would that be? Find the problem with what they own – not enough time, not enough trading power, not enough space – so that you can solve their difficulty with your product.

The purpose of the CLIENT PROFILE is:

- To find the emotional motivators.

- To find any travel problem or a lack of travel and associated benefits.

- To uncover any objections or concerns regarding timeshare.

- To gather information so that you can link it to the uniqueness of your product.

- To build rapport and trust. Without these you have nothing

- To visualize your clients as your newest owners.

- To find out WIIFM (What's In It For Me?) and link the WIIFM to the benefits of your product. Do this after the INTENT TO SELL.

Never disagree with anything your client has to express that is their opinion and not yours. This is very difficult to do because you want to sell. Resist the temptation to sell too early in your presentations.

You have nothing if you don't like your clients or if they don't like you. Therefore, you must find *something* you like about your clients. Once you find this small *something*, your clients will automatically *begin* to like you. This, simply stated, is the law of reciprocity which means: to give and take mutually; to return in kind or even in another kind or degree.

The Three Essentials

Transference of Positive Energy, Likability and Trust

Awaken

Awaken their emotions with emotional motivators; emotional reasons *why* they will buy today.

Sticky note on your bathroom mirror

Have Courage
Be Prepared
Do Not Give Up
Be Positive
Great Opportunities Occur
Just Do It and Go For It!
Anything is Possible
Be Persistent
Be Determined to Succeed
Be Decisive
See it Before it Happens
Wait for the Miracle to Happen!

Chapter 18

4. RECAP

"I AM a very CARING person."

"I AM CARING"

<u>RECAP</u> – Show How Much You Care

The RECAP is nothing less than a comprehensive verbal summary of the information collected from your clients during the CLIENT PROFILE portion of the presentation. It represents a crucial step in the presentation because any misunderstanding about your clients' circumstances and travel patterns can be clarified and corrected if necessary on a timely basis. The RECAP also demonstrates to your clients that you have been listening, and that you truly care about their unique situation.

The RECAP is vitally important because the act of listening shows that you care and are trustworthy. Remember, "People don't care how much you know until they know how much you care." This is one of the more difficult steps to master because you must truly pay attention to how your clients respond to your questions, but then also internalize non-verbal communications that have transpired during the beginning steps.

The RECAP has six parts to it:

1) Associate information with the Five Core Motivational Needs
When you begin to do your RECAP, your goal is to take the information gathered and start tying it back into the Five Core Motivational Needs. Refer back to Chapter 7 to refresh your memory concerning these five items, and why they are so important.

2) What Matters Most
You also want to take the information gathered and tie it back to what you think is most important to your clients. Is it financial security, improving quality time, living a healthier lifestyle, fulfilling dreams and accomplishing goals or feeling wise with their money so they can provide for their family? Start talking about how your clients can move towards accomplishing their needs and desires by improving upon their current situation.

3) Confirm their Emotional Motivator
Ask your clients if you are correct in how you interpreted what they have said to you.

4) Clarify Needs and Desires
Besides the emotional reason your clients would buy, you want to clarify the size of accommodations, the season, or any other program specifics available at your resort that they want or need. Then verify the reasons for your recommendations.

5) Earn Trust by Repeating Back
Within your RECAP, repeat back their names, their kids' names and ages, their jobs, hometown, favorite hobbies, vacation activities, past and future vacation spots, dream vacation and their next planned vacation, and a vacation problem that needs to be fixed. For example, "You told me earlier that you're not spending enough time with your kids and that's weighing heavily on you. The one thing that I can assure you is that this ownership program will help you to spend a lot more time with your children."

6) Forward Moving Statement
End the RECAP with a forward moving statement. "Let's talk a bit about how you and your family would vacation with ownership." Or, "Understanding your family, I believe you'd be excited to hear more about this!"

Be mentally aware, and understand how this step changes the dynamics of your sales presentation. The whole psychology of the presentation is about to change from a focus on establishing the setting to getting into the core components of the presentation. At the end of your RECAP you must keep the end result in mind. A bell should go off in your head indicating "Game On!" All of the discipline, focus, study, confidence and preparation take over and become the deciding factor of the end result. Most importantly, you are transitioning into the next step which is the selling portion of your presentation. Be fully aware that you are beginning to sell at this point.

Trust

A firm belief in the reliability, truth, ability, or strength of someone or something.

The Law of Trust

The *right* relationship between
language, meaning, and the world.

Attraction

The action or power of evoking interest, pleasure, or liking
for someone or something.
A quality, feature or benefit of something or someone that
evokes interest, liking, or desire.

The Law of Attraction

You attract into your life whatever you think about.
Your dominant thoughts will find a way to manifest.

Chapter 19

5. INTENT TO SELL

"I AM the EYE OF THE TIGER and the HEART OF THE LION."

"I AM POWERFUL"

INTENT TO SELL – Amp It Up; Use Passion and Conviction!

Ding! Ding! Ding! The bell has gone off, and now it's time to sell. This is the last step of the foundation of your presentation. The time has come for the tone of the presentation to change. It is time to share with your clients the "Law of the Sale." The law of the sale is to explain how your company conducts its business with buyers today.

Train Your Brain - A very successful concept. Remember a time in your life when you needed to summon up energy. For example, if you ran track, when you heard the starting pistol. If you ever played basketball, remember how you felt when you heard the buzzer at the start of a game. Just remember whatever auditory signal you can recall, where you're actually reliving the moment and actually hearing it in the present, that forces a memory of an adrenaline rush. The adrenaline rush that you are bringing upon yourself is absolutely necessary to change your emotional state. Your clients will see it, feel it and experience it, and they will want what you're showing them because of this energy burst!

Deliver your INTENT TO SELL statement with confidence and outright conviction. It is imperative to have this statement memorized so that you can deliver it without hesitation. The delivery of your INTENT TO SELL statement will tell the real story. Be direct, and make it clear that all interested consumers make their decisions to become owners only during their initial visits.

The INTENT TO SELL statement has seven components designed to make sure that the message conveys a sense of empathy while at the same time capturing your clients' attention and leading the presentation forward. These seven components are:

1) **Time Acknowledgement**: The Time Acknowledgement is a communication technique designed to capture the full attention of your clients so they feel connected to the presentation. It is your acknowledgement that their time is valuable, and that the information provided throughout the remaining portion of the presentation will be valuable to them regardless of whether or not they make a purchase. When people believe there is something in it for them, they are more likely to

listen and actively participate in the presentation. Your clients must have a sense that they will gain some value or insight for their efforts.

2) **Need Statement:** The value of your product must be expressed in terms of its benefits to your clients. These benefits should be directed towards gaining more value for their money and better quality time with their loved ones. In addition, you might present the benefits from a Fear of Loss position, creating the perception that your clients' lifestyle and future goals could be diminished if they don't change their vacation lifestyle.

3) **Greed Statement:** The Greed Statement simply explains the notion that if your clients like and want the features and benefits of the product, you will serve as their advocate, and work with them to find the very best price or deal available today.

4) **Urgency Statement:** All of the urgency is tied into one main thought. The features and benefits of your product are only available to your clients if they purchase on their initial visit. The First Day Benefits should be used as a tool to gain leverage when discussing the urgency of the decision to purchase. Your clients must understand that if the decision is delayed, the product will become more expensive and provide fewer benefits. Why would anyone come back later, and pay more to get less?

5) **Action Statement:** The Action Statement is designed to ascertain whether or not your clients understand and agree with the "Law of the Sale." Your goal is to get a firm, black and white agreement from them that they not only believe, but trust you and the process of the sales presentation. It is similar to when a judge asks in court "Do you understand the charges?" The final answer to that question is always absolutely certain, and never left in doubt. The Action Statement can be extremely direct, or as subtle as "Are you with me so far?" or "Do you understand?" The art of becoming a Master Closer comes down to how well you deal with your

clients' responses to direct Action Statements. Be sure to get agreement from each of your clients individually in addition to agreement as a couple.

6) **Take Away:** Many salespeople think Take Away Statements are as simple as saying "This may not be for you" or "I don't know if timeshare is right for you." In reality, these statements are only part of the story. A real Take Away Statement is much more sophisticated. First, give your clients something they want or need, and get confirmation from them that the value of the feature and benefit is real. Then, retract the feature and benefit so that they understand it is only available if they purchase during their initial visit. The use of a Take Away is essential because it diffuses any pressure. The seven words that can accomplish this are, "Whether or not you buy this today..."

7) **Manager Support:** Because of the parallel technique of the Four Basics, the Front-End Bump has already occurred, and your clients have met your manager. The stress caused by mentioning that a manager will be helping out has already been alleviated. Therefore, it will be a seamless transition to your CLOSE, "Bob and Mary, you remember David..." and reintroduce your manager. The psychology is to have the manager become a familiar face viewed as an ally in helping your client get the very best deal. The last thing you want to do is cause your clients to bring up the objection, "Oh, we don't want to meet your manager, we'd just like to stick with you!" Even worse, your clients might say to your manager, "Are you the *closer*?" Role reversal: *How would this make you feel as a T.O. manager?*

It is absolutely critical that you believe in "The Law of the Sale." Any attempt to think in other terms such as taking a deposit or letting your clients give you an answer in a few days, will be terminal to your career. A timeshare sale is all about now, and will never happen tomorrow. It is imperative to have an undeniable conviction that when your clients leave the presentation, the sales process is over. Salespeople with the powerful ability to turn down a sale and say "No" to a Be-Back ultimately become much more successful than those who don't have that kind of courage.

Chapter 20

6. WHY TODAY / CLUB CERT

"*I AM* not selling timeshare, I am selling *TODAY*."

"*I AM TODAY*"

<u>WHY TODAY / CLUB CERT</u> - The Law of the Sale

It is not difficult to sell someone on the concept of Vacation Ownership. The challenge is to get them to purchase today. The process of moving your clients toward purchasing today should incorporate an "Easy Does It" approach, and should be handled throughout the presentation. There must be an incentive to make purchasing today look much better than purchasing tomorrow – or next year, or when your clients think they will be in a better situation.

The offer of an incentive for purchasing during the initial visit should always be in writing and should be non-negotiable. Rather than a rule which can be broken, your First Day Incentives must be law, and there should be consequences if that law is broken. As a broker, you should train your brain to believe in the law – this will make you stronger. When you explain the First Day Incentives, defer blame to the developer. "I'm just the messenger! My developers offer these privileges as an incentive to earn your business while you are here today."

It is also important to explain it as if it is no big deal. Shrug off any objections to the today law. "Whether you purchase today or not is entirely up to you. If you do join as our newest owners today, you get these extra benefits. It's as simple as that." Once you move to the next part of your presentation, your clients will know, whether they like it or not, that there are definite advantages associated with doing business today. Later in your presentation, when they are moving toward purchasing, they will ask for clarification of the First Day Incentives and the Law of Today. Great questions starts with, "So, if we buy this today…!"

"Everyone's favorite day is *someday*. It is our intention, goal, and purpose to make *someday* turn into <u>*TODAY!*</u>"

~ Nick Cunningham

"You are not selling timeshare. You are selling <u>*TODAY!*</u>"

~ McEneryism

Chapter 21

7. WHY VACATION

"*I AM* a problem solver. I see *SOLUTIONS* for every problem."

"I AM SOLUTIONS"

<u>WHY VACATION</u> – Solve Their Problems With Vacations

The Purpose of Life

Why should anyone spend more time taking vacations? Taking more vacations can give people the chance to spend more time with family and love ones, become healthier, accomplish goals, make dreams a reality or have new experiences filled with adventure and romance. These are all very good reasons as to why people should vacation more, but do they actually need to vacation in order to accomplish these things? Not necessarily.

Taking more vacations does not necessarily directly correlate with gaining more of the Five Core Motivational Needs. As a matter of fact, people do not necessarily need to take vacations in order to accomplish the core needs. How many people have been happily married for 40 or 50 years, and have an amazing relationship despite the fact that they have only taken a vacation twice in their lives? On the other hand, how many people vacation regularly, but then divorce after only five years of marriage because of differences that could not be resolved? What about the father who takes his family camping and motorcycle riding every weekend during the summer, and cannot think of a better way to connect with his children? Vacations do not necessarily provide the ultimate solution to the problems associated with people's efforts to obtain more of the Five Core Motivational Needs.

You can state with good intentions "You need to take more family vacations so that you can be closer to your family," or "You need to take vacations so that you can have more adventure and romance in your lives." It is true that taking vacations can bring families closer together, and give them a sense of adventure and romance, but it is not absolutely necessary to vacation in order to achieve those needs. Essentially, the point is debatable.

What if, instead of saying the above statements about vacations you ask, "If you could spend more time with your loved ones, would you want to do so?" or "Are there people in your lives with whom you would like to spend more time?" How do you think your clients might answer? The most powerful way to explain the benefits of the timeshare product is to first define the objective, and then link the product as a solution to achieve that purpose.

The key idea here is to avoid using the timeshare product to define what matters most in peoples' lives. Instead, define the greatest purpose in life, and then link your ownership program as a solution.

At this point, it is important to philosophically reflect upon life in general, and attempt to understand the real purpose of life. Now, it can be said that nobody actually knows the real purpose of life. However, at the end of the day, the purpose of life can be stripped down to a very simple theory. The purpose and value of life is found in the relationships generated throughout the course of a lifetime.

If someone goes to the doctor, learns they have cancer and only three months to live, what would they do? If someone in this situation could accomplish only a few things within that timeframe, what would be most important? When people find themselves on their death beds, they don't say things like, "Will you bring me my awards and diplomas? I want to see them one more time." Neither do they say "Bring me a list of my assets so that I can marvel at them one more time." When life is ending, people do not surround themselves with material objects. They want to be surrounded with the people they have loved and had long term relationships. When people are dying, they surround themselves with family, and photos of their parents, spouses, children and grandchildren. They reflect upon their most valuable friendships, the things that mattered most in their lives.

At the very end of life, relationships are what really matter the most. It is the relationships, and not the achievements and acquisitions that are the most important things in life. As a result, relationships must have priority in life above and beyond everything else. Try to imagine life without any relationships at all. Would it really be worth living? Wisdom comes from learning these things sooner than later. Do not wait until the end of life to figure this one out. If relationships are so important in life, why do so many people allow their relationships to get the short end of the stick? Unfortunately, people get incredibly preoccupied with making a living, paying bills and acquiring things as if these tasks are the essence of life. Living a balanced life is important, but for most people, is it really balanced?

Most would agree that the amount of time dedicated to a project or relationship is directly proportional to the importance of that project or relationship in their life. In order to learn clients' priorities, just look at how they spend their time. People talk about trying to find time for their children, or making more time for the most important people in their lives. However, they later notice that their children are grown and gone, and that their friends are no longer around. Frequently, people end up saying, "It's too late. I can't get back what I didn't do." Time is the most precious resource. In fact, it is a gift. People can always make more money, but no one can make more time.

This concept of dedicating time for the family is especially difficult for men. Many fathers say, "I don't understand why my wife and kids complain. I have provided them with everything they could ever possibly need. What more could they want?" The answer is clear. They want more personal attention. They want time. Nothing can take the place of personal attention, and the most important concept to convey to clients is, "Why change now?" Most people have important things to get done, and they promise themselves that they will make more time for their families. However, most often, that precious time is never realized. There is no guarantee tomorrow will ever come. Knowing that one day life will end, how can anyone justify that those projects or things were more important than family? With whom should people start spending more time?

Just like Harry Chapin's lyrics in Cat's in the Cradle, "…gonna be like you, Dad, you know I'm gonna be like you," he sings a *Message of Discontent* and a *Legacy of Disconnect*. People need to spend quality time and *quantity time* with their family. Your children do not want presents, they want your presence. Build your relationships and go on vacation, love your family and tell them how much they really matter!

> "But we'll get together then, Dad
> We're gonna have a good time then."
>
> ~ Harry Chapin

It's All About Relationships

The essence of the timeshare product is not about vacations. It's about relationships. Relationships last forever. What truly creates a legacy? The quality of personal relationships is the most enduring impact anyone can leave on mankind. Building lasting relationships is accomplished by spending quality time with the people most important in one's life. It is important to understand that there is a difference between "Routine Time" and "Quality Time." Typical "Routine Time" consists of the things people do on a daily basis such as wake up, go to work, come home, eat dinner, watch television and go to bed. Routine Time consists of things that are done every day, only to be repeated again and again. Quality Time is time spent with loved ones having fun, reflecting on the past, and dreaming and scheming together about the future. It is time spent away from the routine chores of life that matters.

Routine Vs. Quality Time

Life in modern society has become hectic, stressful and fast paced. Both husbands and wives work to take care of their families. Since most of this time is daily routine, when do people take the time to slow down, reflect and truly connect with loved ones to reminisce over the past and plan for the future? It is typically holidays, weddings, funerals and vacations. This is quality time. Three of these four occasions revolve around family which is a good thing. However, most people do not get intimate quality time with their immediate family members during weddings, funerals and holidays. They often get distracted by extended family and friends during those occasions. If someone were having difficulty with their spouse and children, holidays, weddings and funerals do not provide sufficient opportunity to resolve the problems. Only one of the four occasions truly connects people with their immediate family members, and that is the vacations people take as a family.

So why is spending quality time with friends and family so important? This is the time that truly connects people with one another, and it is especially important to spend that time with the people most important in one's life. It is the time that gives a deeper understanding of who they are as individuals and as a family, and what they are all about. Quality time gives people the opportunity to look deeper into their own souls, and the souls of loved ones. It is the time away from routine, mundane endeavors that facilitates new experiences and excitement. It is the time to do the things that have been put off or only dreamed about such as having a romantic dinner, participating in new activities, going on an adventure, or just relaxing and reconnecting the love. A large part of connecting with one another involves looking into the future, and planning life objectives. It's the time to reflect on the enjoyment of past events, and gain joy by anticipating the future. This message must be delivered during the presentation, and then linked through a stage of understanding to how owning a timeshare will help create better interpersonal relationships.

The most powerful way to deliver a message is with conviction. Link vacations as the solution to their challenges or problems.

VACATIONS → QUALITY TIME → BETTER RELATIONSHIPS

Since life is fundamentally about relationships, how can people create great relationships? By spending quality time together. So how can quality time improve? Spending time with loved ones away from the routines of life improves Quality Time. By taking vacations, people can truly get to know each other's innermost values and needs.

The message of the presentation should not be about vacations, but about making choices and having structure so that people can build their most valuable relationships over the course of time. This is accomplished by spending quality time together. Quality time is invaluable. It is the most valuable one-on-one time spent with loved ones and friends that create deep bonds which last a lifetime. Spending quality time with family will give the peace of mind knowing that the right thing has been done. It should not be necessary to look back with regret, guilt, remorse or anger.

Healthy Lifestyle

Let's not ignore the health benefits of taking vacations. There have been numerous studies done over the years that have highlighted the health benefits of taking vacations, and the health problems associated with not taking time away from work and routine life. Higher vacation frequency has been attributed to the better general health of Europeans, who tend to take more vacation time than the average American. The health toll on non-vacationers is more risk of heart disease, poorer sleep, more stress, tension, depression, fatigue and marital strain. While on vacation, people walk more, watch less television, read more and talk to each other more. Most people will also find that they are more productive at work after returning from a great vacation.

Vacationers learn to love each other again! They learn to be grateful for what they have in their lives. Vacationers are definitely more reflective when they're in the moment on vacation. They begin to love life all over again.

People should put effort into their marriages because there are plenty of people who charge a fortune to dissolve them. Remember that they were in love once, so instead of being apathetic, which is the opposite of love, they need to rediscover each other and rekindle their love while vacationing. Rather than dissolve it, reconnect and relive the romance.

The Vacation Commitment

In finding a vacation commitment from your clients, go through a sequence that delivers a message that can impact a broad based group of people.

Securing a Vacation Commitment is absolutely critical to making a sale, but does not necessarily need to be in place at the beginning of a presentation. Many novice sales people will change or stop their presentation if they feel their client is not responsive to vacationing. However, Master Closers can entice clients into feeling the need and urge to commit to spending quality time with the ones they love by relating anecdotes and telling third party stories. A commitment to vacation is something that can be nurtured and developed during the course of a presentation, and could become one of the primary reasons your clients purchase.

Story Time

Your ability to be an effective storyteller is one of the most powerful communication techniques that can determine your success in this business. Using stories helps people connect with the product you sell, and vicariously allows them to experience the value and benefits your product delivers.

The number one delay objection anyone hears in this business is, "We need to think about it" or, "We never make decisions on the same day." Both are a polite way of saying, "No." If during your presentation, you deliver a powerful story about a significant loss caused by a delay in taking action, perhaps the emotional connection your clients feel with regard to your story will have a great enough impact to propel them to say, "Yes" during the course of your presentation.

"Third party stories are not about you. They are about others."

~ Common Sense

"I have helped countless families become owners by sharing exceptional, extraordinary and exciting Third Party Stories."

~ Glenn Brady

Write down your happiest memories with your loved ones:

_____

_____

_____

_____

_____

_____

_____

Did your happiest memory have to do with a vacation? If not, think of a vacation, excursion or a family visit that you hold as a favorite memory.

_____

_____

_____

_____

_____

_____

_____

Chapter 22

8. EXCHANGE

"*I AM* going to turn my clients' *DREAMS* into reality."

"I AM DREAMS"

EXCHANGE – Getaways and Vacation Commitment

SIZZLE the exchange! The exchange system explanation should be the highlight of your product presentation. This is where you put it all together. Create excitement, and make your clients understand that they can, in fact, accomplish their goals and aspirations through vacation ownership.

This portion of your presentation highlights three segments plus an additional Time Out for a private review of the exchange directory. First, justify the value of vacation ownership. Second, explain how the exchange system works. Finally, showcase the quality inherent to the exchange network. Most importantly, emphasize how easy it is to work the system!

Justify the Value: Essentially, the justification of value is a high-level comparative analysis of the cost associated with renting against the cost of ownership. You will use the numbers you gather here in the RENT VS. OWN step of your presentation. Ask for numbers that are real to your clients, most typically an average of their previous per night expenditures for vacation lodging rentals. The price of your product recommendation will be the breakeven point between the amount of money it takes to become an owner and the amount of disposable income your clients will ultimately be willing to spend on your product. For non-affluent clients, the breakeven point might be in the range of $75 to $100 per night. Affluent clients will recognize a breakeven point closer to a range of $200 to $400 per night. These numbers should always be realistic to your clients. Never use numbers above your clients' past personal experiences. Most people cannot grasp the concept of spending $2,000 or $4,000 per night for the rental of properties in the directory because they have never had the personal experience of spending that kind of money on a per night basis for lodging.

Justify the value immediately prior to explaining and showcasing the exchange system because the quality of the affiliated properties will directly impact your clients' feelings about the value of your ownership program. Demonstrate excitement and ease of use of your resort's exchange system. Show resort brochures that express the quality your clients can expect to enjoy through the exchange network. This will move them toward the idea of a better quality of life which happens to be one of the Five Core Motivational Needs.

How the System Works: Give a brief overview of how the exchange system works. Help your clients envision where their plans will take them as owners. Be specific. When speaking to non-timeshare owners, the most important message to get across is the fact that the system is viable. Your clients will be asking themselves the obvious Consumer Concern, "How do we know the system will work for us?" What stops a person quicker than anything is feeling that the money invested could potentially be a waste.

Show the Getaways or Hot Weeks so that you will build value during your presentation. Master Closers will discuss Getaways or Hot Weeks and recognize when to Commitment Trial Close to persuade a *non-owner* of timeshare to become an owner during their initial visit. Your purpose is to Commitment Trial Close when discussing these exceptional properties and these low cost vacation weeks. It is critical that you be intimately familiar with the exchange network, so that you can easily guide them through the directory toward their dreams.

The main focus with *timeshare owners* should be educational. Explain a couple of nuances about the exchange that they may not already know. Demonstrate knowledge of the system in order to gain credibility, and the opportunity to show that the resort under consideration is better and different from their existing ownership.

The Quality of the Network: Showcasing the quality of the resorts, and giving hope that the future will be better than the past, is what makes people willing to change and buy into vacation ownership. Begin with an overview of the overall scope of the exchange network. When showcasing the network, use specific examples from the experiences of existing owners at your resort. Don't just hand your clients an exchange directory, and say "Take a look through this directory, and tell me what you find." Give a personalized verbal overview of the exchange, and show resorts near areas of interest to your clients. Be sure to highlight regional destinations within driving distance of their home. The cost of airfare can become an unnecessary objection. After highlighting regional locations, show some of the more exotic destinations, resorts representing more of a "Once in a Lifetime" experience to round off the fulfillment of your clients' dreams.

Time Out: It's time to give your clients some time to get acquainted with the directory, and to discuss the limitless possibilities of the exchange between themselves. Show them how to use the index to find their destinations of choice. Give each client a directory so that both individuals get involved with the process. Again, give them a task so that their level of interest can be weighed. This step will help determine if further explanation of the benefits is necessary, or if they are ready to preview the property they are considering purchasing.

At this point, ask your clients "What questions have I left unanswered up to this point?" "Is there anything you would like me to clarify before we move forward?" "Do you like what you are hearing so far? We'll visit the property shortly so that I can show you first hand the kind of luxury your family will enjoy for the rest of your lives for the same money or less than you are spending right now if you get involved with the ownership program *today*."

"You will never be younger or better looking than you are today."

~ James "J. R." Roberts

Do not sell the steak, sell the *SIZZLE!*

SIZZLE the Exchange!

SIZZLE SELLS!

SIZZLE!

Sell in Color

Gather several travel magazines and look for the ads that are catchy, colorful and attention-grabbing. Write out what motivates and moves you.

Stunning. Mysterious. Quiet. Hawaii has been all that for centuries!   Serenity!

Fulfill your sense of adventure while awakening your senses! Undeniably alive!

Unspoiled. Uncommon. Unpretentious.   Moments become memories! Indeed!

_____

_____

_____

_____

_____

_____

_____

_____

Chapter 23

9. WHY TIMESHARE / RENT VS. OWN

"*I AM* financial sense. What's a hug worth? *PRICELESS!*"

"I AM PRICELESS"

<u>WHY TIMESHARE / RENT VS. OWN</u> – 14.9% vs. 100% LO$$

The emotional value of vacations should now be firmly in place. Your clients should be cognizant of why vacations are so important to their lives. Now comes the time to explain why timeshare is so advantageous to the stability and comfort of their financial future. This is when the financial logic of ownership can be tied to the realization of dreams. Once again, this issue needs to be presented in two separate and distinct ways. Owners of Timeshare and Non-Owners of Timeshare must be given two different messages.

Owners have already made the leap of faith regarding timeshare, so now the question becomes, "Why more?" When dealing with these clients, it is very important to avoid downgrading or knocking what they already own. Congratulate them on making the decision to get involved with timeshare. Spend 90% percent of your presentation speaking about adding to their portfolio. Don't compete against another resort, and dissuade them from thinking they need to sell their existing ownership before purchasing from you. Your message should be about not owning enough timeshare. It is impossible to win a situation that cannot be controlled, so unless there is justifiable room to negotiate, emphasize the value associated with your clients keeping what they already have in place and adding more to it.

Non-Timeshare Owners need to be convinced that having ownership will accomplish many objectives such as improving their overall quality of life and giving structure to their future. Since they haven't yet taken the leap of faith necessary to become timeshare owners, spend more time on industry credibility and explain how personal growth comes from change. If your clients don't ever change what they are doing, what they're doing will never change.

There are multiple subjects within this part of the presentation that need to be covered in order to deliver a powerful message answering the question, "Why should we buy?" The order of the delivery will be the same regardless of whether or not your clients already own timeshare. Internally they have the same thoughts that can keep them from taking an action step.

First, address why your clients should have timeshare in their lives. Then acknowledge that timeshare isn't perfect. The industry has had some growing pains. Walk your clients through the most important considerations when looking into ownership. Then, follow up with the purchase requirements of your product. Incorporate a forward moving or benefit statement, and finally cover the financial logic of ownership. Master closers compare timeshare ownership costs with a hotel rental receipt, commonly using the term *Anyway Money* as a benefit statement. They are implying that their clients may as well own because when they go on a vacation, they're going to spend the money *anyway*.

The WHY TIMESHARE / RENT VS. OWN step is very important because it shares with your clients the benefits and financial logic of your product. It's a very simple but powerful opening to share with your clients why people buy timeshare. The set up for owners and non-owners is the same, and should be done using the power of numbers. Presenting your point with numbers not only strengthens the message, but also allows you to test your clients by omitting the last item to see if your clients correct you by saying, "You said there were three points to consider, and you only shared two with us. We are curious what the third one might be."

Non-Timeshare Owners

Begin by saying, "Before we get started, I want you to know that there are three main reasons why people become timeshare owners."

- People compare the value of owning to the cost of just renting hotels as they go, and learn that they get much greater value and quality for the same money they were currently spending anyway.

- People become owners because they cannot justify the cost associated with renting the quality of resorts found in the ownership network.

- People become owners to improve the consistency in quality when it comes to enjoying their leisure time away from home.

Timeshare Owners

Begin by saying, "Before we get started, I want you to know that there are three main reasons why timeshare owners buy more time."

- Owners recognize the value of setting up their vacation retirement plans so that their financial security is set by using today's dollars to acquire more property at today's prices.

- While their earning potential is at its best, owners take future rental dollars and add to their portfolios.

- Owners broaden their leverage in the trading networks by increasing the number of properties and the amount of time they have in place for future vacations.

These three points should be memorized for either type of client.

Credibility of the Industry: It's very important to alleviate any fears your clients might have regarding the timeshare industry. Timeshare has greatly evolved from its infancy, but there still exists some stigma concerning the functionability of the product. Use stories, metaphors or analogies to help your clients understand the tremendous growth and value this product delivers today. Be sure to mention the fact that global name brands are now part of the timeshare industry, and that they would not risk their good names with a system that didn't work as advertised.

Timeshare Sense: Talk about what the experts say one should look for when considering making a purchase of a fractional product. Look for a deeded ownership in a highly demanded destination that is not over-built. Location, location, location!

Financial Breakdown: You should be trial closing early and often after your INTENT TO SELL statement. The timing associated with presenting the terms of your purchase proposal is essential because you just talked about what your clients should look for when considering acquisition of the property. Now, you want your clients to start understanding the financial numbers involved with actually purchasing a vacation ownership interest. Break out the down payment and the monthly amount. If there are restrictions to qualify for the developer financing, share them with your clients. At the end, use a Commitment Trial Close to see if they will be using the developer financing, securing their own loan or paying cash.

Forward Moving Statement / Better Quality: After breaking down the financials, reiterate that buying into a fractional property is as easy as simply converting a future travel expense into an asset today and accomplish enhancing their leisure lifestyle while setting up their future financial security. Ownership is all about improving their financial, social, physical, and leisure life. It's a repetitive process, but just keep repeating what's in it for them.

Financial Logic / Rent vs. Own: The Rent vs. Own section of the presentation can be delivered in many different styles but the fundamental nature of the message remains the same. Buying an asset using money spent without a monetary return will financially outperform its alternative. This is the crux of the financial logic. "The most expensive thing someone can buy is something they don't own." Here are three different ways to explain the Rent vs. Own logic. They are:

The Present

One way to deliver the Rent vs. Own message is to use your clients' current spending habits for their vacations. If your clients have been candid and you have a connection with them, using the numbers associated with their current expenditures could offer a real picture as to how much money they are committed to spending over a defined period of time. What you want your clients to feel is the pain of remaining in their current lifestyle. You need to make them understand the fact that without making a drastic change in how they are spending their money, upgrading into resorts of luxury is rather unlikely.

The Future

Another way to deliver the Rent vs. Own message is to forecast what the future is going to look like. This style is very beneficial if your client either doesn't have a vacation commitment or you want to increase the financial number large enough for your client to feel a monetary problem.

When a client doesn't have much of a vacation travel pattern, it's difficult to use past or present numbers. These clients need to understand what the future holds in store for them when they do start traveling more consistently. When discussing this position, you must share with confidence that your clients' travel pattern will change over time. As people get older, they have more free time, and tend to vacation more frequently. In order to strengthen your message, you must use the phrase, "According to financial experts, or according to Wall Street experts...." The information becomes irrefutable when the experts say it. Then, when talking about the numbers, explain your point from a third party position stating, "The average family spends between $75 to $150 per night for lodging. Families who vacation just one week per year will spend roughly $28,000 on lodging alone over the next twenty years after taking inflation into account." Your goal is to create a financial picture that will unfold when your clients start traveling. This now becomes a problem to solve because they either don't have the money required to start enjoying their leisure time, or the financial outlay for ownership you demonstrated was created using modest numbers for modest accommodations when their dream would be to live a more upscale vacation lifestyle.

Some clients are traveling vacationers, but recognize that their vacation lifestyle will change some in the future. They have the money to accomplish their vacation lifestyle today, but will have more free time in the future. Their family will grow in size, their needs will change. Your clients will need larger accommodations in the future. Your goal is to forecast what their future lodging expenses might look like when their vacation time increases, and the quality improves. Forecasting the future has incredible value because the size of the problem will be large enough that they will mentally adjust the numbers. Once adjusted, the numbers become a concrete problem.

The Cost For Quality

Using the Cost For Quality format is a great way to show your clients how consumers are getting much more value for their money with ownership. This is normally done when you are showing the quality inherent to the network of resorts. Top quality resorts in the network on average cost $300 - $500 per night. Without ownership, your clients are unlikely willing to spend the money necessary to stay at this level. What your message says is, without changing how your clients are currently spending their money, it will be impossible to stay at the quality level you are showing. It is very important to remember your trial closing statements because you want your clients to realize they will not be accomplishing their goals if they don't make a change. Use statements like, "Have you ever spent $300 per night of your own money for lodging? If you are not willing to pay that kind of money, how will you ever be able to stay in these types of resorts?"

There are many times during the presentation when it is necessary to take a time out. This serves two purposes. First, your clients need a little time to digest the information presented so far. Secondly, your clients need to have the opportunity for a private discussion as to the merits of your presentation. However, these breaks are for you as well. The sales process is an intensive mental game. You must walk away, and mentally analyze your clients. You must think about their body language, and reactions to questions in order to decide if they are open minded. You must also determine which one is more dominant, and decide which of them may need more attention while gaining commitment to the end result - making the sale.

When leaving clients alone, you should always give them a task to accomplish while you are away. This allows you to gauge their level of interest and see, first hand, which one is more dominant and actively involved in the presentation. Hand your clients a list of reasons to purchase timeshare, use the FIVE IMPORTANT THINGS (F.I.T.) sheet from the next page. "I'd like to invite the two of you to take a minute, and look over this list. Will you please check five things that would be the most important to you if you were ever to purchase into a vacation ownership program? I'll give you a few minutes to discuss this list." If they haven't done what has been asked of them, there is no need to continue. No participation on the part of your clients means no sale.

FIVE IMPORTANT THINGS (F.I.T.)

If you were to ever purchase Vacation Ownership, what would be the five *most* important things to you?

☐ Location

☐ Save Money on Future Vacations

☐ Luxury Accommodations

☐ Amenities

☐ Flexibility

☐ Exchange Possibilities and Preference

☐ Exceptional Management

☐ Safety and Security

☐ Quality

☐ Activities

☐ Ability to Pass on to the Kids

☐ Future Property Value

☐ Freeze Out Future Inflation

☐ Deeded Ownership

☐ Personalized Services

Chapter 24

<u>10. PRODUCT</u>

"<u>I AM</u> going to Keep It So Simple (K.I.S.S.)"

"I AM K.I.S.S."

<u>PRODUCT</u> – Product Recommendation and Worksheet

The PRODUCT portion is the nuts and bolts of your presentation. This is where your clients learn how the product is sold, and how it actually works. While highlighting the strengths of the program, share some of its weaknesses too. If you never tell your clients what the product won't do, it is very difficult for them to believe what it will do. Make sure when explaining the usage, you also talk about what they won't be able to do with it. Nothing is ever perfect. The ownership just needs to be better than what your clients have been doing.

Since your clients just finished filling out the <u>FIVE IMPORTANT THINGS (F.I.T.)</u> sheet, you must now *LINK* what they checked to the product you are about to recommend. If they checked Ability to Pass on to the Kids, how are you going to link that to your product? If they checked Location, how are you going to link that to your product? Yes, some might be more difficult to link than others, so be prepared to make a recommendation with conviction. Preparation plus Perfect Action equals Success! Think through this because it will come up on your tables. It is your purpose to come up with great solutions and recommendations. Knowledge plus *Action* equals Power!

When delivering the information, say it simply and succinctly. Great communication involves getting points across with the least number of words necessary. If you become too long winded, the impact of the information you're presenting will be greatly diminished. It is also possible to inadvertently bring up additional concerns that might have been unimportant until mentioned. Be extremely conscious of wording, and the amount of time it takes to make a point.

Presenting the different unit sizes and ownership packages should be done in a recommendation mode. Start making specific recommendations as to which ownership package might make the most sense based on how much traveling your clients already do, and how many people they will be accommodating. This is not the time to be ambiguous. If your clients have trouble deciding which program they might want and oscillate between options, quickly help them narrow down their thinking until there is a maximum of two choices on the table.

At this point, you have shown the prices. Some salespeople hold back the price until the very end of the presentation. However, this runs counter to normal shopping patterns. When deciding on making any major purchase, most people want to know the price up front so that they can have time to internally ascertain the value and justify the price. When showing prices, break down all the money associated with the purchase including the down payment and monthly installments. With the pricing in mind, your clients will be able to truly determine if the program is worth the money to them personally. While they are thinking about it, present them with a summary of the most powerful components of your presentation, the exchange system and the resort. In this manner, you can truly help your clients determine if the program will work for them.

Concurrent with the discussion about pricing, explain the annual costs of ownership. Ownership dues continue to be one of the most significant Consumer Concerns about timeshare. Because association dues continue forever, many buyers become afraid. Build tremendous value around the homeowner association dues. After all, it is the dues that give ownership interests the foundation of security. Once your clients have the purchase price of the property paid in full, they will be able to secure their future leisure time accommodations at a fraction of the cost associated with renting. All they will have to pay is their pro rata fair share of the property maintenance. This is what creates financial stability because they would otherwise be paying high per night rental rates for lodging which will only continue to increase due to inflation and the profit motive. Emphasize that the homeowner's association itself is non-profit, and is there to protect the value of their initial investment.

"Features, Advantages, Benefits."

~ F.A.B.

"It's not the product. It's the person."

~ U.R. Bonding

Chapter 25

11. PROPERTY/MODEL TOUR

"*I AM* focused and purposeful. My clients deserve *OWNERSHIP*."

"I AM OWNERSHIP"

PROPERTY/MODEL TOUR – Commitment Trial Closes

Use a systematic approach to showing the property. Describe features and benefits using all five senses and all communication devices whenever possible throughout the PROPERTY/MODEL TOUR. When showing the grounds and setting of the resort, be observant of your clients' reaction to the new surroundings and listen to what they say. Be aware of those clients who express complete satisfaction with everything they see. If they express no objections or concerns about the property, there exists a good chance they will not be purchasing anything. Ask if there is anything going on in their lives that would prevent them from becoming your newest owners today.

Overview: Prior to actually touring the property, give your clients an overview of everything they are going to see. Explain what they will see on site, and share information about the various services at the resort. Then, emphasize the consistency of quality your clients will experience with ownership.

On Site Property Grounds: Describe everything your clients see. There should be a set pattern for every PROPERTY/MODEL TOUR. Point out all of the amenities, but highlight the ones that would be of most interest to your clients.

Power Statements: A power statement is a winning, definitive, positive and clear phrase that encapsulates the single idea you want your clients to have about any given topic. It is a call to action. Power statements create an immediate connection with your audience. Get your clients' attention and create trust between you and them.

Examples of Power Statements:

- When you partner with us, you are investing in a company with more than 25 years experience creating great memories for families.

- The only decision you have to make is how you are going to spend the money you are already committed to spending.

- How would you feel if you could check out of a $5,000/week luxury penthouse with a $150 bill?

- If you ordered a mid size car and the rental agent said to you, "Hey, you're the best looking family we've seen all day so we're going to give you a complimentary upgrade to a Lincoln Continental at no additional charge. It's all on us!" How would you respond?

- How do you think owning one of the last ski-in/ski-out developments in town would affect future value and tradability?

- What plans do you currently have in place to protect and assure the quality of vacations you've become accustomed to once you reach retirement and go to a fixed income?

Property Services: Since services are typically an invisible benefit during the PROPERTY/MODEL TOUR, verbally describe the services offered while walking the property.   Share the specific services offered, and highlight the ones most closely aligned with your clients' personal needs.

Suite: Prior to walking into the model, give a brief overview of what they can expect to find inside.   Do this prior to entering the suite so that they can absorb their surroundings without interruption.   Pay very close attention to the body language of your clients.   See what attracts their attention, and remember what they comment about.   See what's important to them.   When the timing feels right, ask a few involvement questions in order to find out what your clients are thinking.   Ask them, "What do you find most appealing about this suite?"   While in the model, always ask if they have any questions.

Closing Question: "Can you see yourselves enjoying this type of accommodation with your family a couple of weeks per year for the rest of your lives?"   "Will the Two Bedroom Winter work for you today?"

"He who speaks first loses, Silence is Golden."

~ Penn N. Teller

Chapter 26

12. CLOSE

"*I AM* in the zone and the *END RESULT*."

"I AM END RESULT"

<u>CLOSE</u> –Welcome Your Newest Owners!

Our intention is to always Trial Close and test the water before the final CLOSE. You should be trial closing right after the INTENT TO SELL. Being a Master Closer, you started with Compliance Trial Closes and moved into Commitment Trial Closes. Study and master Compliance and Commitment Trial Closes because they are the most important techniques of the sales process. You must be able to seamlessly transition between Compliance and Commitment Trial Closes. If your client becomes resistive because you are using Commitment Trial Closes, you should simply switch back into Compliance Trial Closes.

With practice you will develop unconscious competence to move between Compliance and Commitment Trial Closes seamlessly and effortlessly – knowing when to move forward or back off a bit based on your clients' reactions and responses to your questions. You must understand your clients' body language to know when you're pushing too hard. This is where you switch from Commitment Trial Closes back to Compliance Trial Closes. *Easy does it.*

At this step in your presentation, offer to cover any additional questions or concerns regarding usage or affordability, and then ask your clients to buy. "Can I welcome you as our newest owners today?" The most important concept of closing is to continue asking for the sale. If you get resistance, cover the concern, add additional value with either new information or elaboration on the most important points, and ask for the sale again. Closing the transaction is a simple process. Ask for the sale, add more information and once again, ask for the sale.

When your clients give an affirmative response, congratulations are in order. The sale has been made. Proudly welcome them into the resort as one of your newest owners, and shake hands with them. At this point, the sale has been acheived, *so stop selling*. Then describe the following six items related to the purchase process:

1. Estimate the amount of time necessary to do the paperwork. Preserve at least a ten minute buffer for additional questions that may arise.

2. Explain exactly who will be assisting with the paperwork.

3. Complete the paperwork thoroughly, and review for errors or omissions.

4. Describe the upcoming initial service or welcome call to be anticipated from resort staff members.

5. Highlight service aspects associated with the exchange network.

6. Offer to provide personal assistance with any part of the ownership program at any time in the future.

If your clients decline the first invitation to purchase, don't give up. When your clients say "No," find out why, and address their concern. Offer to take a look at the inventory for special pricing opportunities if money is the main objection. Most importantly, continue to sell. Summarize the features and benefits inherent to the program your clients are considering, and emphasize why they should go ahead and proceed with ownership. Reiterate information about any of the Five Core Motivational Needs that appear to be most important to your clients, and review the features and benefits of the product that would add the most value to their lives.

Tie your clients down with statements like, "You told me earlier...." Ask them, "If you knew that this program would do for you what it has done for so many other families, would you give it a try?" Ask them, "Does the (recommended program) sound like it will work for you today?" Ask "If you were to join as our newest members today, what would be the worst thing that could happen?" Then, be quiet and wait for an answer. After getting their response, ask them, "If you were to join as our newest members today, what would be the best outcome for your family?" Summarize the benefits of ownership, and add some new product information or change the terms of the sale. Many clients respond favorably to new information. Then use an invitational close, such as, "Sounds like 'Welcome Aboard'!"

Hold onto a few concessions that you can offer as a final nudge to make your clients comfortable with their decision to purchase. Something like referral or reward dollars to use in the restaurant or spa, a bonus week certificate or owner's cards for their adult children will go a long way toward your new owners' happiness.

During the closing sequence, ask your clients to buy three times. The first time, ask them if the program makes sense, and if they are thinking about getting involved with vacation ownership. The second time, ask them if they are definitely considering having the vacation ownership program in their lives. The third time around, simply give them the worksheet, and ask them to fill out the top section. Leave your clients alone at this point so that they may discuss the merits of the program privately. After a few minutes, come back to them in order to see what is going on. If they haven't completed the worksheet at this point in time, clear the table of everything except the worksheet and First Day Incentives Certificate, and get a manager for assistance. When turning to a manager for assistance, summarize the situation in front of your clients. Give the manager sufficient information so he or she knows exactly how to proceed. Be succinct, but thorough in this regard.

Throughout your entire sales presentation, consistently ask questions that make your clients say "Yes." The questions need to be designed in a format that will generate predictable responses. They must also revolve around the Five Core Motivational Needs. Reiterate that people most often regret things they didn't do rather than things they did do in their lives. Repeat the following statements throughout the presentation, and then reiterate them during the closing sequence.

- Do this for your family, not for me.

- I'm simply showing you how to redirect the money you are going to spend anyway on future vacations in order to get better value for your family.

- I'm here to help you help yourselves.

Most importantly, keep it light, have fun and enjoy a most successful career selling the fastest growing segment of the travel industry – vacation ownership. Changing people's lives for a living is an incredible challenge and a rewarding opportunity.

There are many different ways to ask for the sale. However, the process should be smooth and easy flowing. The best salespeople get the consumer to purchase without directly asking for a "Yes." Study and learn how to apply the following closing techniques, and always ask for the sale repeatedly.

The Summary Close

The Summary Close is simply a reiteration of all the key benefits related to your client and then asking for the sale. You continue to cover the benefits they expressed the most interest in during your presentation.

The Choice Close or Preference Close

This close is simply asking your client to make a choice between two recommendations. This close can either be directed towards the product or indirectly targeted towards the closing process.

- "Would you like to own the annual or biennial program?" "Would you prefer to own the Summer or Winter Program?"

- "Who has the best penmanship?" "Would you like to take ownership as Tenants in Common or Joint Tenants?" "Would you like your payments to start on the 1st or 15th of the month?" "Do you want a Bonus Week or would you prefer Referral Dollars in your account?"

The Cash Close

The Cash Close restates the fact that regardless of whether or not they own their vacations, your clients will spend the same amount of money over the next ten years anyway. Because this is the reality, ownership will offer a much greater value for the same money. Ownership secures the ability to continue traveling in first class luxury for the remainder of their lives and their children's lives.

Give It A Try Close

The Give It A Try Close simple asks the consumer to "Give it a try." Bob and Mary, with ownership, your family will have luxury vacations available each and every year for the rest of your lives. You will have the opportunity to spend invaluable time with your loved ones every year, and you'll get the pleasure knowing your vacation dollars went further with ownership. Why don't you give it a try? What's the worst thing that could happen? What's the best thing that could happen?

The Directive Close

The Directive Close leads the consumer into the closing process by explaining the next step. After you have made your closing statement reiterating the benefits you would say, "And the next step is…." Then proceed with the first steps of your paperwork process.

The Secondary Close

The Secondary Close is asking a closing question related to using the product. "When we deposit your week with the exchange network, would you like it deposited as the whole two bedroom or a one bedroom and a studio?" "Would you like Owners' Cards for your children today, or would you prefer I mail them to you?"

Inventory Price Drop Close

The Inventory Price Drop Close should always be tied back to inventory in a building or phasing of the project. This not only legitimizes the price concession, but also adds scarcity because of the limited number of units available for sale within the special pool. Based on the number of transactions occurring that day, the inventory your client is considering will very likely be sold before the day is over.

Phase Drop

"We are currently selling units in the final phase of the resort. The developer opened up sales in the initial phase earlier this year at a lower price point. Now we are selling out the final remaining units. We have been sold out of many programs in the initial phase for quite some time now, but I will look to see if I can find you the very best offer from our initial phase if you are interested in purchasing. We have only two weeks left in the initial phase and they are "x." If I find the program you want at our opening phase price, you will need to take action today. We have more than 20 agents working today, and this inventory will be gone very soon if it has not already been sold."

Building Drop

Building drops work exceptionally well when a development is built in phases. It legitimizes the price drop because the current building under construction will be sold at the list price and the consumer can come back any time to purchase inventory within that building.

The price drop occurs with inventory remaining in the completed buildings. The justification of the price drop is that the product cost less to develop in those buildings than the development of the latest building. This inventory sometimes comes back and sells the same day because of the lower price point. It is very similar to buying into a housing development where the first house costs less than the final ones being built.

Another technique is to say the developer is willing to sell inventory that comes back in a competed building from owners upgrading for a lower price because he is carrying the loan and association dues and is willing to sell it for less. It becomes a win / win situation. "You get the best, lowest price, and the developers get their money."

Rental Drop

A rental drop is a great way to justify the price discount if the inventory is completed. You justify the drop by taking the full rental value per night times seven nights, and give that amount off the listed price as a discount. One caveat is you must never give immediate use at the resort as that would make the drop illegitimate. How to justify any use would be to offer a Bonus Week Certificate in lieu of use of the property during their first week or season.

Upgrade Position

"The developer has an exclusive inventory pool for owners wanting to upgrade their ownership. There is only one week sitting in this pool for you to get the equity position. Otherwise, I can upgrade you into Building "x", and give you what you paid back toward the list price."

"The developer has an exclusive pool of inventory for owners wanting to upgrade their ownership. There is only one winter week left in this pool if you want to upgrade to a winter week. Otherwise, we can't take back your current ownership. If you want this winter week, you will need to act now because it will be gone soon. We have more than twenty sales agents helping out our owner base of more than 15,000 families."

In-House

"Within the owner inventory pool, we have two left at special pricing. I can sell you "x" Program right now for "y". These weeks will be gone by the end of the day. We have more than 15,000 owners, and twenty sales agents working today."

"Use your knowledge without thinking about it."

~ Unconscious Competence

First Phase Price Drop

"Right now, we are offering a Pre-Construction Discount. We are raising our prices by 5% on "x" date."

Additional Closing Statements

Throughout your entire sales presentation, you need to consistently ask questions that make your clients say, "Yes."

"If you knew we could … and would do that, would you be open minded enough to find out how?"

"If you knew… would you want to give it a try?"

"If I could… would you…?"

Continue To Sell and Close

Go back and re-summarize why your clients should buy today. Cover any of the Five Core Motivational needs you feel are most important to your clients, and the features and benefits of the product that would add value according to how they would use it. Ask your clients if they "*LIKE* it, will *USE* it and can *AFFORD* it."

"You told me earlier…"

"What is the worst thing that could happen to you today?" Then be quiet.

Summarize, and then add some new information about the product.

Sounds like "Welcome Aboard! Welcome to our Family! Welcome Home!"

"Do it *successfully* without thinking about it."

~ Bradd Faxon

Lost Sale Close

The sale is never over until it's over. This is called the Lost Sale Close and works something like this:

"I'm sorry I couldn't find anything that works for you today. I'd like to ask, while you're here, if you could share with me the real reason that you're not joining as our newest member. It seems like the ownership program is a great fit for you and your family. This information will be very helpful to me with regard to my work here at the resort." Then, whatever they say – whatever the reason, sit back with wide eyes, and exclaim, "Is that all?" or, "That's it?"

The effect of your comment will immediately cause your clients to rethink their objection, or to realize that it may not be that much of a problem. And many times, that is the case. Their reason for not purchasing may be as simple as not wanting a credit report run, or not having the full down payment amount available on a credit card. Always try to close once again by linking the problem back to an emotional motivator. Make the problem they just revealed seem insignificant compared to the benefits to their family if they were to move ahead with ownership anyway.

"Yes is the one great final answer."

~ Gordon

"It is a net world."

~ Prophet Profit

"Perfect!"

~ Perfecto

PART III

"THE HOW"

12 STEPS TO SUCCESS

PRESENTATION

"THE HOW"

12 STEPS TO SUCCESS

1) MEET AND GREET

2) WALL TOUR

3) CLIENT PROFILE

4) RECAP

5) INTENT TO SELL

6) WHY TODAY / CLUB CERT

7) WHY VACATION

8) EXCHANGE

9) WHY TIMESHARE / RENT vs. OWN

10) PRODUCT

11) PROPERTY/MODEL TOUR

12) CLOSE

It's as Simple as A B C

Always Be Closing. This is a code that Master Closers live by. From the minute you start talking with your clients, your focus should be on closing the sale. First gather information through questions, and then, after your INTENT TO SELL, begin Compliance Trial Closing. The questions you ask while watching your clients' body language, listening to their responses and watching their interaction with one another, all play a part in getting the sale. Always keep the end result in mind: closing the sale.

If you don't know where you're going, you will probably end up without a sale. Closing the sale starts when you shake hands with your clients. If you wait until the end to start closing, 99% of the time your clients will tell you, "We have to think about it." This doesn't mean you start sparring with them the minute you start speaking with them. It means once you get them excited about the program, you assume the sale and show them how they can purchase it *TODAY*.

It's as simple as A B C when you get commitments throughout your presentation. These commitments should never be missed, or you will have left a door open for them to walk out. There are four steel doors that need to be shut in order to leave the only true reason not to buy – and that's money!

The Four Doors are:

1. Get a Vacation Commitment.

   Why should someone purchase your product if they would not use it? You can't sell shoes to a person with no feet. You need to make sure that either your clients have a desire to vacation annually, or get the commitment that no matter what happens in the future, they will take their family on a vacation each year. "Bob and Mary, with all the bills you have in your life, the house payment, new car payment and kids in college, it sounds like from what you have shared with me that you will still get away and take a family vacation every year, wouldn't you?"

2. Get a Commitment on your Location.

    Why should your clients purchase from your developer? There are thousands of other resorts. You need to know the competition, and their strengths and weaknesses. You need to know what separates your resort from the rest.

3. Get a Commitment on Money.

    People buy timeshare for two reasons: Trust and Value. Trust is built by your personality, but value is built by justifying what someone gets for the dollars they are spending. So how do you build up the value? Value is built by adding up all the benefits that make one product different from the another. If Product A has more benefits than Product B for the same price, one will say there is more value in Product A, and if your clients wanted to buy, they would buy Product A. Throughout your presentation, you need to keep piling up benefits that are important to your clients for the money they are spending to build the value of your product. "Bob and Mary, owning your vacations and having something to show for your money makes more sense than continuing to spend your money on rental receipts, doesn't it?" Then, of course, ask, "Why?"

4. Get a Commitment to Owning Now.

    Obtaining a commitment to purchasing now is the most important concept. Why should someone buy today? If someone likes the product, and they want to buy it, then human nature is to always get the best value for the dollar. This commitment is confirmed when they understand that the First Day Incentives are only available today. If your clients are sold on the program, they will buy today to get the most value for their money. If your clients are not sold, the price and benefits don't matter. They won't buy anytime. "Bob and Mary, since you want to get the most value for your money and knowing the developer is offering incentives to earn your business today, the best time to own would be now, wouldn't it?" "If you were to begin saving money on your vacations, when would be the best time to start?"

Using the Five Senses

Your emotions become your reality. Use your emotions and five senses to sell which is simply transferring positive emotional energy. You must move your clients with your power to persuade by incorporating emotion. Be brave and expressive.

Use great verbiage or *wordsmithing* to describe your resort. Pick your descriptions, adjectives and phrases to make the features and benefits of your resort sound as sexy as possible. What advantages have you sold and *sizzled*?

How powerful are the words you choose? Compare the following:

"We had a great time on Maui, Hawaii!"

Or

"We had a great time on Maui! We spent a week delighting and basking in the Hawaiian sun. Dipping our toes in the warm water and the soft white sand, and feeling the ocean breezes on our winter-weary skin was *"just what the doctor ordered!"* We savor the cultural experiences that have left lifelong impression in our memories! This has been a sumptuous vacation, and thanks to our ownership, an "education without walls" for all of us, especially our children. Life is not only a series of memories, but a series of moments. Thank you for your persistence so that we were able to realize our dream vacation. We are ecstatic with our new vacation ownership, and because of you, we are eternally grateful to have a lifelong travel plan."

Which statement puts you in the picture? Remember your five senses! Touch, sight, smell, taste and sound. Using descriptive words to stimulate each of the senses goes a long way to putting someone in the picture, or tapping into their emotions. Of the examples above, which description would make you want to vacation in Hawaii?

EMOTION = ENERGY + MOTION = EMOTION

Come up with a word that brings a positive image to mind. Then use a thesaurus to find three or four different ways to say the same thing. Use all of these words. Expand your vocabulary!

You must spice up your speech through *wordsmithing*.

Delicious: appetizing, scrumptious, mouth-watering, delectable.

Exciting: thrilling, exhilarating, moving, electrifying.

- With ownership, temptations are constantly around you. Venturing off doing something you have dreamed about, taking in the culture and art festivals or searching out your favorite activity. All around, everyone is doing something fun, something you just have to do. Then at the end of the day, the relaxing opulent space of your suite invites you in for the evening and possibly a new adventure awaits.

- With ownership you begin to enjoy the pleasures of your own private network. The simplicity of planning your next vacation comes with personal service. With visions of a warming sun, a fragrant tropical breeze or the crisp clean air of a mountain getaway; these experiences are both exhilarating and rejuvenating and unfold at whatever pace you please. These are the destinations found throughout the premier exchange network.

- From sipping a drink under a seemingly hand-painted twilight sky to whatever the special moment, it will be yours to discover and yours to remember forever.

- This will become the reconnection to understand them better or the ability to give back and surprise someone you love. Trusting the benefits and value of ownership will only enhance the life you currently know. Change is the future.

- The travel revolution is here. Forget everything you have grown accustomed to. You are about to discover Interval International (RCI). They represent a new paradigm, a lifetime experience that consistently has revolutionized the current state of thinking in offering the greatest savings and value in making dreams become reality.

- Interval ownership invites you to experience the new level of opulence in staying in villas and suites previously only open to the ones willing to spend the money. Inside the directory, the resorts and rooms are the same, only the price is drastically different. Over 2,000 are available and just an exchange fee away.

- Who knows what the future holds? With ownership, consistency, quality, space and security become the new standards.

- Our developers want their resort to be synonymous with exceeded expectations and signature service. Our team continues to uphold our commitment to creating your great vacations.

- You can look around, but the difference is crystal clear. Our awards speak for themselves.

- At our resort we offer more room to breathe, to roam, to savor the comforts of home.

- Ownership has given consumers the ability to expand their mind to a creative world picture. It continues to deliver the luxury one deserves and grows accustomed to.

- We have turned our attention to you. You reaching your goals of stability, financial security and consistent luxury have become the cornerstone of our success.

- When it comes to traveling with vacation ownership, the hardest thing is saying goodbye.

- With vacation ownership, there are thousands of ways to have fun.

- With ownership you can follow your passion for extraordinary travel experiences.

- With all the luxuries of home, owners say there's no place else they would rather be.

- With ownership, you'll discover destinations first hand. Everything from authentic cuisine, spa treatments, activities and even architecture to help you feel and experience the native culture.

- Ownership is your insurance package to the life you deserve to look back on and say "I've done what I set out to do."

Let's talk a little about voice. Using the most descriptive, inspiring language in a monotone voice will not get you anywhere. Have you ever heard a great joke told poorly? Not as funny, is it? Speak in the positive with enthusiasm, curiosity and emotion! Have you ever listened to your voicemail greeting and thought, "Hmmm, that doesn't sound like me!" It is eye-opening to watch a video of yourself speaking. It is a great way to self-correct – look for signs of nervousness, insecurity, lack of confidence or insincerity. Watch your body language. Your goal is to be as natural, friendly, animated and confident as if you were telling a friend about a great movie.

Again, your words are your tools. Instead of saying, "When you *buy* this", use, "When you *own* this", or "When you *acquire* this." Be a master wordsmith! Look at these word choices:

Instead of:	Use:
Sign here	Approve this
Cheaper	Less expensive
Down payment	Initial investment

Use positive words for your trial closes and your final close such as prove, easy, result, proud, trust, value and quality. A Master Closer is a perfect wordsmith. Learn what you want to say and how you want to say it before you are with clients. Do your job from the inside out, and always strive to get better at using language to the best of your ability.

Product never sells Timeshare. I don't care who you work for or how great you think your product is, it is NEVER the product that sells. It is always *you* who they buy. If product did sell, anybody could sell timeshare and we would all be order-takers. Please put extreme effort into yourself and your craft, love what you do and the money will follow.

"Never Practice in the Game"

~ Beyond Reproach

On the next page we have overlaid THE FOUR BASICS onto the 12 STEPS TO SUCCESS for your review and study. (THE FOUR BASICS are *italicized*.)

"THE HOW"

12 STEPS TO SUCCESS with THE FOUR BASICS

1) MEET AND GREET

2) WALL TOUR

3) CLIENT PROFILE

Basic 1   *Front-End Bump (end of CLIENT PROFILE)*

4) RECAP

5) INTENT TO SELL

6) WHY TODAY / CLUB CERT

7) WHY VACATION

8) EXCHANGE

9) WHY TIMESHARE / RENT VS. OWN

Basic 2   *Conference (prior to PRODUCT)*

10) PRODUCT

Basic 3   *Worksheet (end of PRODUCT)*

11) PROPERTY/MODEL TOUR

12) CLOSE

Basic 4   *T. O. Management Closing Assistance*

          (Turn the table with a positive and exciting RECAP)

Chapter 27

1. MEET AND GREET

"MASTER CLOSERS have the ability to turn strangers into friends.*"*

<u>MEET AND GREET</u> - Create Fun

The MEET AND GREET can last anywhere from three to five minutes. This warm up is critical because this is where you begin to build the trust and rapport necessary to engage your clients in a good, honest conversation about how, when and why they vacation.

The techniques below are essential in order to help you establish a good first impression. It's critical that you make a good impression in the first few moments that you're with your clients because first impressions are lasting impressions. You only get one chance to make a good first impression. People buy from people they like.

When you first meet your guests, be ready to greet them with a handshake and a warm, friendly and sincere smile. One of the most common mistakes sales associates make in the MEET AND GREET is they start the conversation off in a business context. For example, an inexperienced sales associate might start the conversation with a question such as, "How did you hear about our resort?" Instead, ask your clients about their current vacation, give them a sincere compliment, take notice of the information on the profile sheet to find commonality and share information about yourself. Talk about whatever makes your clients feel comfortable to help relax them. So, how do you make a good first impression?

There are eight components of a great first impression.

1. Initial Contact: There are four non-verbal items going on within the first five seconds that will set the tone and position of your clients' first impression.

- Smile: Show a soft, warm, sincere and friendly smile. When someone smiles at you, your natural reaction is to smile back.
- Direct Eye Contact: Direct eye contact conveys trust.
- Hand Shake: Extend your hand to your client and mimic their handshake.

- Body Posture: Your posture is in direct correlation to your own emotional self image. Keep your thoughts free and clear of all exterior challenges.

2. Give a Sincere Compliment: People want to know they're appreciated, and like to be acknowledged. Try to find something you genuinely like about your clients and share that with them. It's hard not to like someone who's being nice to you.

3. Use First Names: People love hearing their names. Using your clients' first names puts you on a personal level with them. You should use their first names at least three times in the first few minutes. This will commit them to memory so that you can use their first names throughout the presentation. When asking a question or making a statement directed at one of your clients, use their name. This will demonstrate respect, and allow you to establish a trusting relationship.

4. Find Commonality: Selling is a relationship process. Before assuming control, a bond needs to be established with your clients. One of the most important parts of the sales process is the development of this bond or rapport. This connection is created through a feeling of commonality. Use your survey sheet if it lists activities, or look for sports logos on your clients' clothing. Maybe their kids are the same ages as your kids. Find something that you have in common with your clients and mention it. People like people like themselves. However, keep your purpose in mind; every time you say anything, ask yourself if your questions and statements are relevant.

5. Building Rapport: All successful sales are based on rapport. The rapport factor in selling doesn't mean you have to be your clients' best friend within the first few minutes. However, people will not buy from you until they are convinced that you are acting in their best interest, and they will not follow you, or respond to your suggestions, unless they have rapport with you. So take as much time as needed when you first meet your clients to build a strong and relaxed relationship. The very best salespeople have the ability to quickly build rapport with their clients. Your clients must feel that you understand their needs, desires and values.

6. Match and Mirror: Experts state that only seven percent of communication comes from the words stated. The remaining 93 percent is how you say the spoken

words and your physiology. Matching and Mirroring is a very advanced technique that takes a commitment to learn and master. It is called NeuroLinguistic Programming. It will be helpful for you to study these advanced persuasion techniques further. Many excellent books exist to help propel you to the advanced professional sales level. Mirroring and pacing produces a sense of comfort in your clients. Copy your clients' physiology and body language cues.

7. Talk About Yourself: Creating trust is the cornerstone upon which all sales are built. Trust represents one of the most important elements of the persuasion process. One way to establish trust is to reveal something about yourself. Briefly share your background, and the reasons you have chosen to align yourself professionally with the resort you represent. Comment on the quality of sales agents and service personnel attracted to your resort. This helps create trust, and a sense of anticipation and urgency.

8. Getting "Yes" Momentum: Within the first few minutes, start asking questions that you know will elicit a favorable response from your clients. You want your clients to start getting used to saying "Yes" to simple basic questions because as you progress in your presentation, you will start asking more challenging questions. They need to get comfortable answering questions in a positive way.

Remember, the clock is ticking as soon as you say hello. Be respectful of the fact that the only commitment you have from your clients is 90 minutes of their time. Every minute your presentation exceeds that 90 minute commitment is a minute of your clients' personal time. You risk sales opportunities if you are long winded. Only use what time is needed, and don't talk past the sale.

In the Lobby

Introduce yourself to your clients. Ask them, "How is your vacation so far?" "Has your stay in town been enjoyable?" The introduction should be light and friendly. In the first few moments, bond and connect with your clients by finding commonality. Use information from the profile sheet to help initiate conversation. Find something you honestly like about your clients so that you can give a sincere compliment. People like people who like them. Also, remember to use your clients' first names so that you can speak directly to them during your presentation.

1. Where do you folks live?
2. Do you have any children?
3. Have you been enjoying your vacation?
4. What has been the best part of your vacation so far?
5. What plans do you have for the rest of your time in town?
6. What are you doing for fun?

Personal Information

Tell your clients some basic information about yourself. You can do this now or wait until you are sitting at your desk prior to the CLIENT PROFILE, depending on ease and circumstance. Try to link personal information about yourself that would be interesting to your clients. Be as relevant as possible to their lives and their time in your town. For example, ask, "What has been the best part of your vacation?" Attempt to relate something they have done to your personal experiences so that you can establish commonality. Try to find something you like about them, and associate it with your personal information. However, do not go into too much detail here, but give your clients enough information about yourself so that they will feel comfortable sharing information about themselves with you.

Order of the Day

"Most people have a few questions about the presentation when they first arrive for their tour. They usually want to know, "How long is this going to take?", and "What are we going to do?" The first thing I would like to do is take a few minutes and talk with you about how you and your family like to vacation, where and what you like to do, what quality you justify spending your money on and determine how much money ownership can save you. Then I will explain and show you how the program works, share with you some great incentives we offer and then, go see the property."

"Picture a brick wall.
Imagine taking the bricks down one at a time.
Your purpose is to remove all the bricks.
Now the playing field is level."

~ A. Beginning

"Find something you like or *love* about your newest owners."

~ Life is Good

"Let the healing begin"

~ G. Will Hunting

Chapter 28

2. WALL TOUR

"MASTER CLOSERS believe in their company and product."

<u>WALL TOUR</u> - Build Excitement

Proceed to the Resort Model and position your clients facing you across the display.

"Our resort was designed with the idea that the best things in life should be right out your front door. The resort is located 50 feet from the newly located Independence Super Chair and the new $25 million gondola. Directly in front of the resort are some of the best groomed intermediate runs on the mountain. From this chairlift our owners can access the complete ski experience ranging from beginner to double diamond runs. When we go up to the resort, I will point out the mountain terrain so you can see what I'm talking about."

"We have a full restaurant and a piano bar, complete with fireplaces and a beautiful waterfall. All of the concrete outside of the resort is heated. Our owners can enjoy a meal or beverage on the deck area and wave to their friends and family as they board the Independence Super Chair. Near the restaurant is the Business Center and Board Room. Directly adjacent to them is the Aquatics Center with an indoor-outdoor heated pool, kiddie pool, sauna, steam room and fireplace. Our owners can swim from the inside of our resort, out to another pool area and access several hot tubs."

"As you can see, some of the hot tubs are configured as a lazy river so that our owners can float between them. Many of our hot tubs have private areas, and waterfalls connecting them. We also have private movie theatres, an underground grotto and a 3000 square foot day spa and workout facility. We also provide several gas grills. The resort includes a stop for the town bus and a boarding area for our own private shuttle services. Most of our owners take the gondola to and from town since it's free and offers amazing views of the continental divide."

"Our owners have deed and title to this property on the mountain in one of the top ski destinations in the world. In real estate, location and timing can create an invaluable investment."

"The experts say one of the most important attributes to remember when looking at an ownership program is the supply and demand for the area. Breckenridge has captured the title over the past several years as the most visited ski area in the

United States. The properties surrounding the resort range in price from $2.8 million to more than $4 million. Readers of national ski magazines also voted our town the #1 Ski Resort in North America. What this means for our owners is unbridled exchange possibilities within the network. I will talk more about that a little later." Invite your clients to sit with you for a few minutes at your desk.

After you have built a relationship, put yourself in your clients' shoes and ask them what their concerns and expectations are upon coming on the tour. Develop responses to those questions. Communicate your understanding of your clients' point of view by sharing with them exactly what they have been thinking. The Empathy Statement is a skill used to introduce your clients' concerns. Use phrases such as:

"You may be wondering...."

"Many of our guests come in here curious about...."

"A lot of folks come in here not knowing what is going to happen..."

At this point in time, many guests have some very common questions that should be addressed. For example, they may have the following questions, so address these things to ease their minds:

"How long will this take?"

"What's required of us?"

"Will there be any obligation to buy anything today?"

"What if we do want to buy something today?" ☺

Always treat your clients exactly as you would want to be treated. Your kind consideration will alleviate any perceived pressure that your clients may be feeling or anticipating. Be kind and be purposeful!

Magic: The power of apparently influencing the course of events by using enhancing and enchanting forces.

"Magic is believing in yourself, if you can do that, you can make anything happen."

~ Johann Wolfgang von Goethe

"Manifest your magic."

~ McEneryism

Chapter 29

3. CLIENT PROFILE

"MASTER CLOSERS gather golden nuggets."

<u>CLIENT PROFILE</u> - Listen and Gather (No Selling Yet!)

Open-ended questions are questions that cannot not be answered with a single word or phrase such as "Yes" or "No." Open-ended questions help build rapport and encourage your clients to give their input and elaborate.

Open-ended questions…

- Minimize defensive responses.
- Show the speaker's interest in the listener's ideas.
- Communicate an openness – freedom from right or wrong answers.
- Are more likely to stimulate conversation.

Open-ended questions typically begin with…

- What… Tell me…
- How… Give me an example…
- Who… Explain…
- Where… Say more about…
- When… Tell me more…
- Describe…

Open-ended questions elicit trust, respect and honesty. These questions are designed to discover, to ask, to draw out and to explore. Be curious and be a facilitator rather than an interrogator. Your clients should want to answer!

Closed-ended questions bring forth a yes or no response. Use these questions sparingly during the CLIENT PROFILE. These questions are more appropriate during the selling portion of your presentation after the INTENT TO SELL.

Is this… Will this…

Do you… Are you…

In a perfect CLIENT PROFILE, you will get to deeper, emotional questions that elicit emotional responses. This can be challenging. Not every client will accept phrases such as "How does this make you feel?" "Why" questions without trust will be viewed as defensive in nature and create a wall between you and your client.

After the INTENT TO SELL and much later in the presentation, once the privilege has been earned, you must ask emotional questions, such as, "How does that make you feel?" and "Why" questions. At this point, direct, suggest and provide answers for your clients.

"Okay Bob and Mary, if it's alright, I would like to discuss your vacations and free time. Can you tell me a little about how and when you currently vacation and spend your free time?"

Once you get the basic information, you need to proceed to the more emotional conversation. Begin by asking the following:

"Do you consider vacations a luxury or a necessity?"

"On a scale of one to five, five being very important and one being you could live without them, how would each of you rate vacations?"

"How do you currently vacation? Hotels, condo's, staying with family?"

"How many timeshare presentations have you been on?"

"What prevented you from acquiring an ownership in the past?"

"If you were ever going to own a fractional or vacation ownership program, what would cause you to do it?"

"How many vacations do you take per year? How many mini vacations?"

"Why are vacations important to you?"

"If you could change anything about the way you are vacationing now, what would that be?"

"Okay, Bob and Mary, next I would like to discuss what you like to do while on vacation, alright?"

"What type of activities do you like to do while vacationing?"

"Can you tell me where you will probably go that's a little more local or realistic in the next few months?"

"If you won the lottery and time and money were of no concern, where would your dreams take you?"

"If you totally fell in love with this, is there anything that would prevent you from becoming an owner with us?"

Past:

- "You wrote down you vacation "x" weeks per year. What do you typically like to do with your time off?"
- "What type of accommodations do you prefer to stay in?"
- "Do you generally travel with friends or family, or is it just the two of you?"
- "Where did you have your last presentation?"
- "Thinking back to your last major vacation, what is your best memory?"

Present:

- "If you had a place in the mountains, is there a time of the year you would see yourself using it more or less?"
- "Is there a time of year that is easier or harder for you to take vacations? Why?"
- "When you think of the reasons that vacations are important to your family, what comes to mind?"
- "When you hear the word timeshare, what are the first three things that come to mind?"
- "Are you big planners when you book a vacation, or are you more last minute and spontaneous?"

Future:

- "Are there places you have wanted to go to that you have not yet been?"
- "If you could change anything about the way you are currently vacationing, what would you change? Why?"
- "Thinking of places closer to home, where would you go within driving distance?"
- "Where do you dream of vacationing?"

Chapter 30

4. RECAP

"MASTER CLOSERS do not care how much they know until they know how much they care."

<u>RECAP</u> - Show How Much You Care

"Okay, Bob and Mary, you both have challenging careers in the medical field, Bob as a physical therapist and you, Mary, as a pediatric nurse. You enjoy taking an annual vacation to the beach, and you also enjoy our town for hiking and biking activities. Bob, what's important to you is adventure. You enjoy exploring, hiking, snorkeling and any adventure that excites you. You are more of a thrill-seeker than Mary. Mary, you enjoy relaxation and to you, that means quality time with your two children, Kyle and Ashley. You watch them in the pool having a great time while you read and have a drink. Your kids are three and five, and Bob hopes that when Kyle gets a little older he takes up the same activities that he likes. The biggest benefit here is that you already have Kyle and Ashley on skis, and you would love for skiing to become a tradition for your family.

You told me earlier that you enjoy nice places because of the safety and security they offer your family. You have been to Mexico several times and the problem you had there was that the brochure was quite different than the accommodations. You feel timeshare may be a better alternative because of the consistency of quality accommodations. Your dream vacation would be going to the South Pacific as a couple, but while the kids are still young, you are planning a sunny vacation in Florida this summer.

So if I could show you a way to have a lot of fun, realize some of your hopes and dreams that you shared with me earlier, that would be exciting for you, wouldn't it?" (Ask Bob and Mary separately, and get agreement from both.)

"Take that to the Bank!"

~ McEneryism

The RECAP is the most unused, undervalued, left out and left behind method in our industry. Remember, the RECAP shows how much you care. Your newest owners do not care how much you know until they know how much you care. The sale is made right here, right now, because you have truly listened and repeated back what is ultimately important to your newest owners. How many times in your life when you really needed someone to listen to you, and understand you, were you disappointed? They let you down! When they did not listen, did you feel frustrated, angry and disappointed? This is a time to improve all of your relationships! All relationships are based upon feeling heard, understood and valued.

Chapter 31

5. <u>INTENT TO SELL</u>

"MASTER CLOSERS have an undeniable spirit."

<u>INTENT TO SELL</u> - Amp It Up! Use Passion and Conviction!

This is where you must change your emotional state to a high vibration frequency of positive energy in order to change your clients' emotional state. It is time to share the fun. Let the game begin! Ding! Ding! Ding!

Assuming that your clients are ready to proceed with open minds, the examples below demonstrate Commitment Statements. However, sometimes your clients might be non-engaged, annoyed or irritated. You must have the wherewithal to draw on empathy which reduces tension, by beginning your INTENT TO SELL with Compliance Statements, ("our owners", and "they"), and then transition into Commitment Statements and Commitment Trial Closes ("you").

"What I'd like to share with you is a wonderful way to vacation with your family. Maybe this will give you a little inspiration to think about travelling more and staying in amazing places. As we go through the possibilities of what vacation ownership offers, I ask that you keep an open mind and an open heart. (The greatest distance that we all must travel is between our head and our heart.) We understand that this is not for everyone, and may or may not be right for you. If you decide it's for you then I will welcome you aboard as one of our newest owners. However, if you decide it's not for you, *it's not for you, simple as that!* Is that fair?" (Shake both husband and wife's hands.)

Passion and Enthusiasm Statement

"I feel that you will be very glad you took the time to discover what ownership at our resort will do for your family. The program I will be introducing you to is one of the most flexible in the world regardless of whether you pay rent in the future or become an owner with us!"

Your Strongest Positioning Statement

"Today, you are going to be introduced to a very special program. Our intention is to earn your business for life....not just your lives, but also your children's and grandchildren's lives. This will have to make sense for you in your mind and in your heart. It's that simple."

"Please look closely at what I'm going to show you. It will be up to you to decide if this is for you or not. My goal is to present a different and better way to vacation while creating a greater value for the vacations you want to take *anyway*. My intention is not to pressure you in any way. However, you will know in a short time whether this makes sense for your family or not. If it does, great! If not, that's okay too. Any pressure that you might feel is internal because *you just might want one* (laughter)! So, are you ready to get started and have some fun?"

At this point your clients should feel comfortable, relaxed, open-minded and intrigued with what you are going to share with them today.

Change Direction

At times you cannot be rigid to your script and you must do something unorthodox or entirely different. Salespeople must change their sail (sale) when the wind changes. Change is in an instant, always initiated by you. Only you control your presentation. Here is an example of extreme change and redirection.

If your clients are still nervous or uncomfortable, repeat some of the earlier dialogue, so that you can use this precious time for bonding. Spend one or two minutes talking about their family, work or vacation, and then segue into your background and family with a two minute overview. This will build a relationship through casual, non-invasive conversation. All successful sales are flowing, stress-free and relationship oriented.

Personal Information

Show your pictures.

About Us

Talk about your company's culture. Talk about being the "Brand Name" in your town.

Company History

"Our company has been a family owned and operated business for more than 25 years. Our developers are Mike and Rob Millisor, and Mike Dudick who joined them as a partner in the late 1990's. Their first resort was on the east side of town and since 1998, they developed and sold out our second resort on Peak 9, and were chosen by Vail Associates to help develop the Peak 7 Base Area and our newest resort.

"We are rated as a Premier Resort with Interval International, the leading vacation exchange company in the world. They have more than 2,500 resorts in 65 countries, and most of the major hotel brands including Marriott, Hyatt, Westin, Embassy and Four Seasons are a part of the system."

Our Success

"Our company has been the recipient of numerous local, national and international awards for excellence in product quality and services. The American Resort Development Association (ARDA) named us as the 'Project of the Year' in 2003 beating out all other resorts in the industry. Since 1999 we have achieved more than 30 national awards from ARDA recognizing the company and its employees for exceptional service and performance. We have also won the ARDA award for being the #1 employer in our industry. In addition, our company has won numerous local awards for ethics, superior customer service and outstanding generosity for giving back to the community. Let me assure you these awards are not given out lightly and when we win, we are extremely proud of them because we have become the best in sales by being the best in service! We could not have won the customer service award unless the product has met and exceeded the expectations of how people wanted to use the property. No other company has been able to match our recognition and performance to date anywhere in the Rocky Mountains. With this type of national and international recognition, would you feel comfortable doing business with a company like ours?"

Community Service

- Explain how your company contributes to your local community.

- "… and our company's motto is "Always great vacations.""

- "Next I will give you a little idea of who we are. We have been in town for over 27 years, we sell $50 Million a year, have over 14 thousand owners, and have won over 70 industry awards. We are also one of the top development companies in the county."

Our Community

We have received the Better Business Bureau's highest rating awards including the business of the year several times. We have also earned also received Ethics Awards for the way we treat our guests. The company has also received several awards for philanthropy, most recently, for donating more than $100,000 to the Summit Foundation for helping disadvantaged families.

Current Press

- Use articles relevant to your resort and area.

- "During talks to develop a resort at the base of Peak 7, Vail had a list of names ranging from Marriott to Hyatt to potentially work with them, but they chose us. What do you think that says about our reputation?"

- "Recently an expansion of the ski area to Peak 6 has been in the news quite often. When this becomes a reality, Peak 7 will be sitting in the middle of the newly expanded ski area. Your timing couldn't be more perfect. When the final news broke about the Gondola, values at Shock Hill doubled overnight! I will point out Shock Hill when we drive over to see the resort."

- Analogy: Having accomplished these awards against all the major brand names is like starting a coffee shop and within a short time becoming as well known as Starbucks, or starting a software company and having it rival Microsoft.

"Bob and Mary, I would like to take a few minutes and answer any questions that you may have up to this point." When you're ready to move on, there are many ways to deliver your statement of INTENT TO SELL.

Statement of INTENT TO SELL

"Folks, the first thing I would like you to know is whether you buy one of these today or not, the developer would like me to show you a different and better way to spend your vacation dollars and get more value for the money they know you are going to spend anyway. At our resort, it's all about giving people more value for their money than the alternative of renting. However, with that said, they recognize that owning a vacation ownership property isn't for everyone, and our resort may or may not be for you. So today, I'm going to talk about a great way to vacation and save a lot of money doing it."

"We sell more than $50 Million a year, and have more than 15,000 owners. None of them expected to buy anything as they walked in for their tour, but every day this company sees people just like you come in thinking, "No", but once they understanding who we are and what the product does, one out of three becomes an owner at our resort because it is so different than other programs out there. If after previewing the resort, you would like to learn more about the additional benefits and value of the property, I will find someone to help you get the very best deal possible."

"The developer knows people like you don't come in expecting to fall in love with what they are offering, so in an effort to help those families take the leap of faith into their program, they have put together an incredible incentive package for those families who purchase during their initial visit."

Statement of INTENT TO SELL

"Bob and Mary, this presentation is for you and your family. It's to learn about a different and better way to spend your vacation dollars and get more value for the money you are going to spend anyway. At our resort, it's all about giving more value than the alternatives. However, with that said, we recognize that owning a vacation ownership property isn't for everyone, and this may or may not be for you."

"So today, I'm going to show you how people are shifting their buying into this type of second home. We sell $50 Million a year and have more than 15,000 owners. Every day people just like you come in with no intention of purchasing anything. Once they understand how much better and different we are, one out of three do become owners, *today*. If during the presentation you like what you see, I will work to find the very best program that fits your needs and search the inventory to give you the very best price. Our Developers have a great incentive package to earn your business today if you like the resort."

Statement of INTENT TO SELL

"Our intention is to earn a customer's business for life. Not just your lives, but also your children and grandchildren. That's a big statement. There is only one way we can expect to accomplish that… by creating a greater leisure value that cannot be experienced without us. It's that simple. If you believe, as our other owners do, that this value is real, and your ownership with us can significantly enhance your lifestyle, then the only thing that separates you from benefiting will be the courage to take advantage of our invitation to join us today during your visit. Are you prepared to keep an open mind and have some fun?"

"Before we get started, I'd like to go over the bribes with you so you have time to think about them. Because we are a sales organization and we know we only get one chance to meet with you, we do our best to earn your business while you are here. Once you go home, we know we'll never see you again. So we have some bribes to encourage you to do business while you're here today, if that makes sense."

"All of these come with your ownership if you get involved today. These are not for tonight, tomorrow or next week. I'll just go over the first three because these are usually the most important to my owners."

Go over the three most important of your First Day Incentives.

"Can you see yourselves using any of these?" Or, "Would any of these be useful to you? Which ones? Why?"

"Just to show you in writing, these incentives are offered to you during your initial visit which is during your tour. These incentives are from the developers only. If the green light starts flashing, then it will be an easy decision anyway. Are you with me so far?"

"Our time together will be directed toward vacation ownership, and what it will do for your family. If this is for you, great, buy it, and if not, that's okay too. As for high pressure, we sell $50 million a year and we don't beat anyone over the head to do it. About one in three couples become owners with us so it is not for everyone, but it is for some. With that said, would it be okay if we started by talking a bit about how you and your family would vacation with ownership?"

Understand it is your sole responsibility that your clients believe you 100% that they must buy today. They may not like it, but, they must believe it in order to experience fear of loss.

"The basic premise of NeuroLinguistic Programming is that the words we use reflect an inner, subconscious perception of our problems. If these words and perceptions are inaccurate, as long as we continue to use them and to think of them, the underlying problem will persist. In other words, our *attitudes* are, in a sense, a self-fulfilling prophecy."

~ N.L.P.

Chapter 32

6. WHY TODAY / CLUB CERT

"MASTER CLOSERS assure that the big print giveth and the little print taketh away."

WHY TODAY / CLUB CERT - The Law of the Sale

The examples below demonstrate Commitment Statements and Commitment Trial Closes. However, you must have the wherewithal to draw on empathy which reduces tension. *If necessary*, begin your WHY TODAY/CLUB CERT with Compliance Statements, ("our owners", and "they"), and then transition into Commitment Statements and Commitment Trial Closes ("you"). This is the art of selling.

"I would like to take a few minutes and explain our Club Membership Certificate. This is the incentive my developers offer those who purchase on their initial visit. The developers know the best time to earn your business is today, so they are putting their best foot forward today. Now, if you were to become owners with us, when do you think we will give you the very best opportunity to do so?" (Wait for "Today").

"These Club Rights transform this ownership into your private second home. As a Club Member, you now have the right to use the property anytime of the year regardless of what ownership program you buy. Let me share with you the Club Certificate."

"Please look at the first item, Resort Privileges. You get owners' key cards that allow you to freely come and go when you choose. It's your property, and you can use it when you want to. You can take advantage of the parking, use of all amenities on site: the day spa, restaurant, movie theaters, pools and aquatics area and the piano bar. The difference here versus other ownerships is the quality of services and amenities at your disposal to enjoy with your family and guests."

"The second benefit as a Club Owner is Bonus Time. Bonus Time lets you buy additional nights throughout the year at ridiculously low prices. Owners take advantage of these nights for a quick one or two night romantic getaway or some adventure with the family. Because your ownership has compelling value in the exchange network to trade, owners will use these nights back in here at their home resort. What time of year would you use them?"

"The third item is our "Club Points" benefit. This benefit is what truly turns the resort from a standard timeshare into your own private second home. It is simply the easiest way to enjoy real flexibility, and come when you want to. This exclusive privilege for our Club Member Owners allows them to experience their ownership year round, and design their vacations around the different seasons."

"And lastly as a Club Member, you receive impeccable service. Whether you're coming home to visit or you want to receive travel related discounts, you only need to make one phone call and our team will do the rest."

"Do you see the value in being a Club Member versus just owning another timeshare resort? Buyers every day just like you decide to become Club Members because it changes the ownership into your own vacation program."

Collateral Material

Show collateral materials that coincide with your company's First Day Incentives. "By adding this ownership to your portfolio, you get access into the newest type of ownership privileges. How does this sound so far? What is beginning to appeal to you?" Ask both of your clients to answer independently!

"Just to show you in writing, these are offered to you during your initial visit, and are exclusively from the developers. But remember, if this isn't right for you, it doesn't matter what incentives the developer offers. Are you with me so far?"

Please understand it is your sole responsibility that your clients believe you one hundred percent that you never let someone come back. They may not like it, but they must believe it and experience the fear of loss. Your conviction here will make you more successful than any other technique. You must believe your clients will never come back to purchase at a later time. If your clients are obstinate, say "No big deal, my developers have asked me to show you this Club Certificate. They sell more than $50 million a year this way, and they won't deviate or change this successful business model. I am only the messenger, so let's move on." (Blame your developer!) Later in your presentation, get back to the Club Certificate and ask your clients if they understand it, and if they can *conceive* why we do business this way. Do they *believe* it? Then later, when they want one - when you have sold them, ask how they can *achieve* it. Answer: "By buying today... Welcome aboard." Master Closers tie everything to their developer's First Day Incentives which is the Club Certificate.

Link what is most important to your clients to your Club Certificate. Start by mentioning a problem they shared with you earlier, and then show them how they can solve that problem through your Club Certificate. Put this benefit into terms that are personal for your clients, and then tie it down with a Commitment Trial Close in the form of an open-ended question.

The Libby Family

Jason and LJ, do you remember when you were telling me that in your busy schedules it is nice to get out of the house for the day and head up to the mountains to spend quality time together without all the obligations of home?

Well, a feature of the Club Certificate is Day Use and the benefit of Day Use is that the two of you can get away from Denver, come up to Breckenridge where it is 20 degrees cooler and be able to take a light hike and enjoy the fresh air.

The benefit for you is that after your hike, it gives you a home away from home... a destination where you can come back to your resort and relax by the pool, take a shower and then go out and grab a bite to eat feeling refreshed, relaxed and rejuvenated from your day before heading home.

If you had this benefit, how often do you feel you would take advantage of it? Why would that be important to you?

The Fagerstrom Family

Jake, remember when you mentioned that one of your favorite activities is skiing with your son, Beck, but you hate sitting in the I-70 traffic afterwards?

Well imagine being a Club Owner at our resort and having Day Use.

You have a parking spot at the base of the ski area in a heated underground parking garage, and a locker room where you and your son can put on your ski gear and store extra hats and gloves. Take the elevator up to the chairlift and play all day. And no matter who is hungry, cold or tired, you would have something for everybody only 30 feet away from the chairlift at your second home in Breckenridge. You could fire up a grill for dinner, have s'mores by the fire for dessert and then sit in a hot tub instead of the I-70 parking lot.

How many more times would you come up in a month?

How would owning here today improve your valuable family time?

In the previous Linking examples the flow is:

1. Do you remember earlier when you were telling me…

2. A feature of owning at our resort is…

3. The benefit to you is …

4. Commitment Trial Close … (remember to use "You") *page 93*.

"Everyone wants to go to heaven."

~ Not Today

"Yesterday is history; Tomorrow is a mystery."

~ Today

"Tomorrow's not guaranteed. For it to happen, it must be *TODAY!*"

~ Mogi

Chapter 33

7. WHY VACATION

"MASTER CLOSERS have positive energy and power."

<u>WHY VACATION</u> - Solve Their Problems with Vacations

At this point you should know the emotional reason your clients would buy a vacation ownership. Use this to segue into the WHY VACATION portion of your presentation. This section of your presentation is critical because it is in this area that you get the vacation commitment. If your clients are not committed to vacationing and do not understand the benefits of vacationing, then discussing timeshare and its benefits is pointless. Selling timeshare to someone and leaving out the importance of vacations is like making an apple pie and leaving out the apples! Vacation ownership causes families to commit themselves to vacationing on a regular basis. As with many products, people buy timeshare primarily for what it does for them and the way it makes them feel.

Why Vacation

"Before we discuss timeshare basics, I would like to spend a few minutes reviewing some vacation basics, okay?"

Earlier you were telling me that:

- Spending more time off with your family is important so that you can improve your relationship with your kids before they finish school and move out on their own.

- Spending quality time away from work enables you to recharge your energy and makes it possible for you to be a better employee, husband, parent, etc.

- Taking a vacation is a necessity because if you didn't do it on a regular basis, you would lose your mind.

- Taking time away from work with your family enables you to disconnect entirely from the stress that causes you to worry too much.

- Spending time off enables you to feel less stress, and will help you live longer, healthier lives.

- Having fun away from home makes you feel like a kid again, and helps you relive some of the experiences you miss the most from your childhood.

- Traveling is an educational experience that helps you remember to look at the world objectively, and be thankful for everything you have accomplished.

"Here are some points from some of the most popular and well read sources that directly relate to exactly what you were telling me."

Statistical Studies:

"USA Today - 43% of workers polled admitted the biggest mistake they made with their last vacation was not taking enough time off."

"Harris Interactive Study shows that the average employee in the United States takes only half the vacation days of the average European. With most people getting two weeks off, how many total days of free time do you think you have each year?"

"Would you have guessed more than 100? That's a lot of time, isn't it?"

"This is an article entitled 'Extend Your Life' from Smart Money. If you are looking for a reason to take a vacation, here's the best one: It's great for your health. Is there really anything more important? We meet people from all walks of life here and the number one most recurring thing we hear from people who buy our product is that it helps them have more fun and live healthier lives."

If you have a workaholic client, you may want to use the article from HEALTH magazine or FAST Company.

"Earlier you were telling me you like to solve your life and work problems while taking time off. Here is an article from HEALTH magazine you may find interesting."

Health

"Try using a summer getaway to rethink your work situation and make plans for a happier, more energetic future. How to beat burnout," HEALTH MAGAZINE.

Fast Company Article

"Taking a sabbatical doesn't have to mean chaos after you say bon voyage. With the right levels of planning and trust, your absence will only make your staff grow stronger."

After discussing this article, talk about the small amount of vacation time US citizens receive and compare it to other developed countries. With weekends, holidays and vacation time, we all have the ability to have three to four months off each year *if we took advantage of it.*

Why Ownership

"If you are asking yourself, 'Okay, I agree vacations are important, but why should I consider vacation ownership?' you are not alone. Only one out of every three couples we meet with actually purchase, but everyone one of them do so during their presentation. I will tell you more about that later. Here is the vacation ownership concept: If you are going to continue going on vacation each year spending your hard earned dollars to rent accommodations, you may want to consider stopping the hemorrhaging of money each year to the landlords of the world and redirect that same money into a vacation ownership program."

Nicer Accommodations

"Along the way you will not only stay in accommodations that are much larger and nicer than you are used to, but you will have many more amenities. You will control the quality of your accommodations with consistency no matter where you vacation."

Inflation

"And will not be subject to inflation."

Deed is an Asset

"Instead of throwing tens of thousands of dollars down a hole in rent money you will never see again, with vacation ownership you will own an asset that you can sell or pass down through your estate."

"How does that sound? What part of that concept do you like the most?"

"If I could show you a program where you would spend about the same amount of money as you will spend anyhow and give you these benefits, how would you feel?"

Why Vacation Ownership

If your client is considering a second home, be careful not to ridicule their decision. Gently show them how our program may be able to extend and enhance their second home purchase in the mountains through the Club Membership with the following points:

1. Use as overflow lodging or as possibly a rental income.

2. Use the shuttle as temporary emergency transportation to and from the home to almost any place in town or to and from the resort

3. Entertaining (Point out the average $600K second home has zero amenities, no pools, spas, hot tubs, Jacuzzis, saunas, movie theatres, concierge, restaurant, bar, business center, gondola, slope side parking, waterfalls, spa, or workout facilities.)

Do not forget to ask your clients if they plan to stop traveling to other destinations if they buy a second home. If they continue to travel elsewhere, vacation ownership will enable them to get the same benefits.

"Okay, Bob and Mary, are you aware of the trend that has begun this year? You're not? Well let's take a few minutes to review what has been happening." Pull out the Land Title Pie Chart and ask your clients, "If you had to estimate what percentage of the total money lent in Summit County our little fractional product represented, what would you say?" If they are confused, tell them, "Our average sales price is $30,000, and the average second home is $600,000. With that in mind, wouldn't you say that we would probably be a very small portion of the overall money lent here in town? What would you say if I told you we were the LARGEST lender of money in the county? What does that tell you? What we are seeing is more and more families deciding to keep more of their money, and looking for ways to spend less to get more. Comparing a $1.3 million home that requires a $300,000 down payment, and an $8,000 per month payment that usually gets used less than 30 nights per year to a $50,000 total investment that includes year round access for around $100 per night and free Day Use forever, is a large difference. It is a large difference not only in startup costs, but with ongoing long term capital outlay and reduced risk."

"With a second home in the mountains you would be responsible for 100 percent of the purchase as opposed to our program where you only purchase what you will need. By the way, the property next door to our resort is $1.3 million. Which one makes more sense?"

Your children: "Remember that time when…"

Your thought: "My family is growing closer, and moments are becoming memories. Thank God for the memories!"

~ Gratitude

Chapter 34

8. EXCHANGE

"MASTER CLOSERS are dream makers."

EXCHANGE - Getaways and Vacation Commitment

When you start talking about the exchange and how it works, you should have a good idea of where your clients would like to go on future vacations. You should spend exciting time showing them the ease of use and how to successfully exchange into the resorts they would like to visit. The second most common objection people have for not purchasing is that they don't believe the exchange network will get them into the resorts of their choice. You must assure them otherwise.

"Interval International is the premier vacation exchange company with more than 2,500 resorts worldwide. It is a membership only company that specializes in making it easy for owners to exchange from one resort to another. All you have to do is make one simple phone call to access the system. The Westin, Four Seasons, Wyndham, Hyatt and our resort are all part of Interval International."

"When you buy right, trading takes no more time, and is no different than how you currently make vacation plans. But, when people own lower caliber resorts, trading can become much more complicated. We have reached such a premier level in the network over the years that today we facilitate the exchange for our owners directly instead of sending them to the network. All you need to do is call us, and let us know the three basic things you would need to determine for any vacation experience."

"Where would you like to go?"

"At which resort or resorts would you like to stay?"

"How many will be traveling with you?"

"Your exclusive Interval staff here on site will work to fulfill your goals and dreams. It's that simple with us. After they have fulfilled your request, you pay the network an exchange fee and the confirmation is set. There are no additional fees or costs, and no hotel tax."

"Do you remember when I shared earlier the things you should look for when deciding what resort you may want to own? What were the most important features and benefits? That's right, own a Premier Resort, own deeded real estate in an area that cannot be over built, but most importantly, buy the very best location."

"Let me show you." Open up the Interval International Directory to page 14. "Interval International used to let anyone trade for any property. There was no separation of priority. However, when the big developers like Starwood, Four Seasons, Hyatt and Marriott first started participating in the interval ownership world, they wanted the industry to guarantee that their owners would have a certain standard of quality in the industry as it related to trading power."

"They didn't want an owner from a less desirable resort trading into the best ones if they weren't of equal or greater quality. Hence, the Premier rating and demand ratings were established. They're the best of the best. If you own a top rated resort, you can trade straight across to all of the other top ownership resorts in the world. If you want freedom in the network, you must own resorts like ours."

"Over the years, Breckenridge has become one of the most popular ski resorts in North America. That has given our owners global access to the network. Let me give you an example of the quality and flexibility of the network.

Exchange

- Kauai, Hawaii (Show photos of Kauai)

- "Becoming an owner here with our Club Membership will allow you to call our 'One call does it all' number connecting you to your personal travel concierge for all your exchanges."

- Marriot Kauai Beach Club

- Photo Gallery

Resort Directory

Read the resort description. Be sure to emphasize rain forest, lava sand beaches, waterfalls. "The Marriott stretches along scenic Kalapaki Beach where you can swim in crystal clear water. The resort also has a spectacular 26,000 square foot swimming pool with world class amenities. The villas start at 800 square feet and come complete with separate living and dining areas, and gourmet kitchens."

"How would it make you feel to spend a week at the Marriott Kauai Beach Club for the $150 exchange fee?"

As a second example, show your clients the Ka'anapali Beach Club located on Maui, Hawaii in the online exchange directory.

"Ka'anapali Beach is one of the most picturesque beaches in the world, made famous by crystal clear waters, wide white sand beaches and frequent whale pods that jump and dive just a few hundred yards off shore. The Maui experience is exceptional. The Ka'anapali Beach Club offers personalized concierge services, and will arrange everything from surfing lessons to whale watching, dining on some of the freshest seafood known to mankind and private snorkeling tours to Molokini Crater. You can rest assured that when you dial our toll free number, you will be provided with professional exchange assistance from your own personal vacation counselor. Sit back, relax and let us do all the work. We make vacation exchanges as easy as picking up the phone."

Rocky Mountains

- Hyatt Grand Aspen

- Photos of resort

"Selling at more than $150,000 per week, the Hyatt Grand Aspen is one of two premier ski in ski out destinations in the Rocky Mountains." If your clients ask what the other one is, say "Us!" "As you can see, the Hyatt Grand Aspen is right on the mountain. Each residence is impeccably decorated and highlights elegant mountain inspired interior themes incorporating stone, solid wood, granite and marble. The suites have 900 square foot living areas where no cost was spared in catering to some of the most discriminating skiers in the world. Each unit has a complete gourmet kitchen with top of the line appliances and granite countertops. The dining area has seating for eight around a 15 foot mahogany table. Each of the bedrooms are private 800 square foot master suites. Bob and Mary, how much do you think it would cost to rent something like this during ski season, per night?" Do not let your clients evade this question. "Would you ever spend $X per night for vacation accommodations? That's about what these accommodations would cost?" Use the number your clients guessed the suite would cost. Look at your clients and ask them, "Would you ever spend (their number) per night to stay at the Hyatt Grand Aspen? How would it make you feel to check in and out for your entire stay for a small exchange fee? On one side of the hall may be a renter spending $10,000, and you would be spending $150. Which family would you rather be? Do you see now why so many families have chosen to own this program I'm showing you? How long would you have to think about it to make a reservation for $150 for the week?" If they say, "Immediately," respond by saying, "That's exactly what I am asking you to do here today."

"Studies show that people purchase Vacation Ownership because they desire to vacation. *Sell the Exchange!"*

~ Imagine That

"You can't take it with you, leave *memories* behind."

~ King Tut

Chapter 35

9. WHY TIMESHARE / RENT VS. OWN

"MASTER CLOSERS build value."

WHY TIMESHARE / RENT VS. OWN– 14.9% vs. 100% LO$$

Vacation Ownership

Show the articles you have which may be important to your clients.

"I would like to share with you the four main reasons people become owners with us."

- Control: People want to take back control and use their ownership to provide consistent high quality vacations.

- Value: People want to get more value for their hard earned money.

- Financial Security: People want to feel more secure by investing their money back in themselves so that their family gains financially.

- Freedom: People want the freedom to use their ownership when and where they choose, and we provide the full support for ease of use.

"Bob and Mary, which ones would be most important to you?"

"Knowing that each family is unique in their own interests and needs, I would like you to take a few minutes to look over this list of reasons people purchase vacation ownership". Then present your clients with the "Five Important Things," (F.I.T. Sheet) from page 181, and let them mark the reasons most important to them.

"Over the past three decades, the timeshare industry has changed from a once tarnished industry to today's leading choice for vacation property ownership. Fractional ownership offers all the same benefits without the financial stress of buying a second home. The marketplace has changed. People want more freedom, choice and services when it comes to enjoying their lives, and fractional ownership has become the answer. At our resort, we have truly redefined ownership and offer more value than all other alternatives."

RENT VS. OWN

Financial Sense: The RENT VS. OWN is a delicate part of your presentation. Listen to the answers your clients give you. No interrupting, ever, but especially during this step. It is very easy for your clients to feel strong-armed during this portion of your presentation. The numbers you use must to be based on their numbers and their vacation style. Otherwise, they will not find the information credible.

"I would like to take a few minutes to show you why so many people like yourselves become owners. It's the same reason every brand name from Marriott to Hyatt have moved into vacation ownership. They realized logically and financially, vacation ownership just makes sense."

"Have you gone through an exercise before looking at how much traveling really costs you?"

"According to financial experts, going through an exercise like we are about to do together is key in finding ways to become more financially secure. Additionally, knowing how much things cost allows you to become more savvy as a consumer. As a result, you'll get far greater value for your hard earned money."

"This exercise takes very basic numbers of how much you spend for vacation accommodations, and projects how much you will spend on rent over time if you don't own your vacations. It's the exact same method used to determine how much an investment will grow over the course of time."

Travel Expense Summary

"How many vacation days do you take each year?"

"What do you usually spend per night for accommodations?"

"How many more years do you plan to take vacations?"

Use their numbers but guide them to a higher number of years.

"What do you think the annual inflation rate will be for lodging? Bob and Mary, do you agree that costs continue to increase over time? In the travel industry, hotels and similar costs have risen on average 12 percent per year, so with your permission, can we use this number to see how much it could cost you."

"While on vacation, how much does your family spend each day on food?"

Our best brokers will use a summary close and state, "If you're going to spend over thirty thousand dollars in your lifetime on vacations, you should really consider this while you're here." Some will use a chart showing future rental costs and get a commitment from their clients on the amount of money they would spend anyway... *anyway money.*

The purpose of RENT VS. OWN is not necessarily to show your clients how much they will save, it is to show them how to take control of their future expenditures. Have fun with this and challenge them to guess what the acronym of R.E.N.T. is: Return of Equity Not to the Tenant.

Show your clients how to get more value for their money and spend more quality time with their loved ones in the comfort of beautiful, clean, safe and secure accommodations. Remember the five "C's": castles, chalets, condos, cabins and cruises. Allow them to feel the pain of the alternative of cramming a family with children into a small hotel room. Remember the five "B's": bed, bureau, bathroom, bible and the bill. Keep your tone light and humorous, not mean-spirited.

"Bob and Mary, if this is all that you do per year over the next 'x' number of years, you will most likely spend something around 'x.' Does this surprise you? Do you believe this number? The problem owners had when they learned of this number was knowing that no matter what, each vacation meant more money out of their pocket. They realized it was only going to continue getting more expensive over the years. Staying a renter meant the cost was never going to end, and rent would only get more expensive."

"The problem with this number is you will only get what you are willing to spend your money on. People today are looking for ways to get much greater value for their money. People are looking quality, services and greater flexibility. They want to get more for the money they are going to spend anyway."

"What people want is luxury living when it comes to having a great vacation. Let me ask you, what would you expect to pay for a luxury resort?"

"Here's the thing about the cost. What you will most likely spend is 'x' or something close, but to get more (define more to them, more space, more luxury, more amenities) the only option is to spend more money. Would you be willing to justify the money and spend this much?"

"What's great about ownership is this. For the same money you are currently spending or perhaps less, you can get into the lifestyle that would otherwise cost you 'x.' Through ownership, you get the resort on the mountain or on the beach, you get to do all the activities you enjoy and live as if you had this type of money to spend. You get to live a different life than you have today."

Spending the Money Anyway

"For the same, if not less money that you are already spending, through our ownership, you get to live and stay in your own private residence. And unless you change the way you're spending your money, you can only get what you're willing to pay." At the end, explain that it is 'anyway money' and people want more than a receipt for their money, don't you agree?

Summary Close

"When clients decide to own with us, they look at the decision and weigh it against their current spending pattern. They ask themselves, "What will it cost us to get involved, and more importantly, what will it truly cost if we don't?" As you can see, the truth will lie somewhere between these two numbers. If you continue your current lifestyle and since this snapshot is for only x years, the other question to be considered is, "What will it really cost you over your lifetime?"

Chapter 36

10. PRODUCT

"MASTER CLOSERS know that it is you that they purchase."

PRODUCT - Product Recommendation and Worksheet

"If you ever decide to own a fractional program, make sure to buy a high quality premier resort, own the deed and title, and buy in a low supply high demand area. The most important attribute to vacation ownership is where you purchase your home resort. What are those three key words in real estate again? Location, Location, Location! Your resort needs to be in one of the very best locations in an area with limited supply and very high demand. Colorado is known throughout the United States for being home to some of the most popular mountain resorts. Within Colorado, Breckenridge has been gaining in popularity through the years, and today, has become the most popular resort town in the Rocky Mountains."

"In Breckenridge, there are thousands of condos quite some distance from any chairlift, but there is only one property that is within 50 feet of the Independence chairlift and is ranked one of the nicest timeshares in North America. On an annual basis, more people visit Breckenridge than any other ski town in Colorado. The most important consideration is where the property is located. May I ask you, 'If you were to take your family on a vacation to Hawaii and stay in a nice resort, where would you want the resort to be located?' On the Beach! That's right. When people come to vacation in the mountains with their families, where do they want to stay? On the mountain! That's right. Demand is created by the location of where your property is situated, and our resort is located right on the mountain! This determines everything regarding how well your property will trade with other resorts in the system."

"Our product is very simple. We sell a fractional interest in a condo that would sell for more than $1.5 million. We sell fee simple ownership that lasts forever. It's just like owning any property. However, with interval ownership, you purchase only the time that makes sense for your lifestyle and budget."

"Our residences come in 1, 2, 3 and 4 bedroom configurations, and have a lock-off mechanism that will enable you to split a larger unit into multiple weeks. To use your week, call one time up to a year in advance. You can use your week, bring friends and family, trade to more than 2,500 other destinations, or rent to generate income. You can sell it at any time, or will it to your family for future generations to enjoy. There is a one-time purchase price, and an annual maintenance fee. If you choose to use your week elsewhere, you can join Interval International for $99 per year, and if you trade your week you would pay a $150 trade fee. What questions may I answer for you? Do you have a preference for seasons?"

If your clients need more detail, use the following verbiage, but only if they need clarification.

Usage: "As property owners you will have the right to use the property 365 days of the year. It's like having a private country club in the mountains. However, please remember, Day Use is one of the Club Member benefits we offer today. Also, the week you own floats within the season you own, but you will not be tied to the season you own. With Interval International, you can exchange and go anytime throughout the year."

Loan: "Since you own the property, you can have anyone come with you, or if you are feeling generous, you can offer it to anyone you like."

Will: "This property is one of your assets which will not only hold its value in the future because it is slope-side property in one of the most demanded resort towns in the United States, but it will be passed down to generations to come so they can live the same high quality lifestyle they have grown accustomed to by traveling with you. Your grandchildren will be benefiting from choices their grandparents made."

Rent: "One of the great options associated with owning property is the ability to rent it out from time to time and be able to put money back in your pocket if you choose not to use it one year. We do have a management company on site that will rent it for you for a 40 percent fee. However, you can rent it on your own and save the fee. This is a benefit of ownership, but not the primary reason to purchase. You don't purchase timeshare to make money. You purchase timeshare to save money on the rising costs of hotels because you know you are going to spend the money anyway. Basically, the product is free because you are using money you will spend on rent anyway to purchase something of value."

Sell: "Down the road if your lifestyle totally changes and you are not able to vacation anywhere anymore, you can sell the property. Seldom do people want to sell because if they do, they have to go back to renting which is what they are trying avoid. Renting lacks the financial security of ownership. Renters are not guaranteed the quality of their future vacation lifestyle. Renters can only hope they can afford to go one year at a time. How much are your rental receipts worth right now? If you had to sell the property in twenty years, would you only sell it for what you paid and give someone else the equity increase, or would you sell it at market value and keep the profit? Do you think it is going to be worth more or less in twenty years owning property on the mountain in one of the top vacation destinations in the world?"

"If you do sell your ownership at some point in the future, and only get what you paid say 20 years from now, how much would you have saved over the 20 years since you first invested?"

Product Recommendation

At this point, it's time to make your product recommendation. You need to present the main advantages of your recommendation, days of use, size, price, interest rate. Write out a worksheet with your recommendation.

Transfer tax

First Usage

First Payment Date

Interest Rate and Term

Method of Down Payment

Monthly Payment

Once you have filled out the worksheet completely, you need to ask your client the following questions:

1. "How does this look to you?"
2. "Is the monthly payment affordable?"

3. "How about the down payment, is that comfortable?"

    "What type of credit card would you use for the down payment?"

4. "If you fell in love with this program, is there anything that would prevent you from becoming an owner today?"

If they give you any objection, you must isolate on it and ask, "Is there any other reason that would prevent you from coming aboard today?"

"Next, we will review how our program works based on the product you may want to consider owning."

Time Out

Take a time out, and give your clients a task such as viewing Owner Testimonials.

Owner Testimonials

"Okay folks, would you please take a few minutes and read these letters that are testimonials from some of our owners?"

Leave your client alone for a few minutes while they are studying your owner testimonial letters. This is a special time for bonding; a heartstrings moment!

"Timeshare"

~ Sharin Time

"Your deed is your legacy"

~ The Kids

Chapter 37

11. PROPERTY/MODEL TOUR

"MASTER CLOSERS know that nowhere can be now here.
Perception is reality."

PROPERTY/MODEL TOUR - Commitment Trial Closes

Power Statement #1 (Drive through the Shock Hill roundabout)

"This is Shock Hill, one of the nicest neighborhoods in town. These condos to your left sell for $1.5 million which is about $1300 per square foot. The Fairmont, one of the world's top luxury residence clubs is building condominiums here starting at about $1,000 per square foot. The Gondola is just a people mover to get you to the slopes. That Gondola is not ski-in ski-out nor is it a chairlift. That Gondola is taking you to Peak 7 where our resort is located right on the ski slope at the Independence Superchair. If you like this, you will really like what you are about to see!

Power Statement #2 (At the Peak 8 base area)

"These buildings are just the beginning of $100 million playground. There are more than 65 units already built here that start out at more than $1 million, and that's for a one bedroom condo. This is the only place in the world where five lifts converge at one property. Whether you are looking to go shopping, skiing, mountain biking, or hiking it's all here. The Alpine Slide is here as well. In the winter you will have convenient access to one of the top ranked terrain parks in the world! By the way, this terrain park is frequented by some of the top snowboarders on earth. Many Olympic and X Game athletes train here. This area has been ranked as one of the top terrain parks in the world by Snowboarder Magazine. We are only a two minute gondola ride away from the most exciting and exceptional area on the mountain.

Power Statement #3 (Outside the resort)

"There is no public parking access in this area. This is a private, members only parking area, and only those who own here and their guests are permitted to park in these garages."

- Point out Crystal Peak Resort next door, "These condominiums are almost completely sold out. They are all priced over $1,200 per square foot."

- Point out lift and proximity to our resort.
- Point out the indoor and outdoor pools and slides.

Park in the roundabout, and walk directly to the double doors, and up the stairs to the lobby, and ask your clients, "How does the property look so far? If you decide to join as our newest members today, you will be able to use all of these amenities any time you like, including the private movie theaters, the indoor/outdoor pool, the indoor hot tub, three outdoor hot tubs, and the beautiful underground grotto with state-of-the-art water elements. Every aspect of our resort has been designed to impress even the most discriminating buyer. It doesn't matter if you're looking for a resting spot after skiing extreme terrain at the top of Peak 8, or just want a quiet safe haven from the weather with your family. Our Club Membership is designed to give you everything you need to make your entire family have extremely memorable experiences at one of America's top ski areas. You'll be able to view your family skiing or sledding just a few feet from our hot tubs, pools and restaurant/piano bar."

"May I ask you, what do you think those families all have in common? Well, they were all just like you. They probably didn't come here with a plan to purchase, but after seeing the property and its location and quality, they had the courage to move forward with our program on their initial visit. All I want you to realize is that if you decide to come aboard today, you will not be doing anything strange or be the only family who has done that. One out of three of our clients purchase during their sales presentation, and if you decide to do the same, you will be in good company.

Power Statement # 4 (Standing in front of the ski lift)

"Have you ever been at the right place at the right time?" If they say yes, respond, "Tell me more!"

If you could have known what you know now about Vail, and it was 1965, what would you have done? If you could have known what you know now, and this was Aspen in 1972, what would you have done? Where do you think you are now? Are you going to be one of those people that are going to wish you had taken action, or glad that you did?" If they say anything other than glad they did, respond, "It doesn't get any better than right here, right now."

"May we take one of our condos off the market for you?"

"May we welcome you aboard as our newest owners?"

"Will this work for your family today?"

"As I mentioned earlier, we are currently selling Phase 4. If I could find you phase 3 pricing on a unit, would you be interested in reserving one today?"

Linking Statement

Link the emotional reason(s) your clients would buy to our product, and then ask an easy Trial Closing question. Use their first names. Bob and Mary, you told me earlier that you love the mountains! Can you see why we have so many owners just like you? This is an easy Compliance Trial Close.

Linking Statement

Your purpose is to link their emotional motivators back to your Club Membership. Prior to entering the model, pause and say to your clients, "Do you remember your last vacation, and the accommodations you stayed in? I want you to visualize those accommodations and remember as we enter, if you choose to come aboard today, the benefits you will enjoy with the Club Membership. You will be able to rent this room using Bonus Time at highly discounted rates. You will be able to exchange this suite for like kind all around the world. The best part is, if you desire to rent additional weeks above and beyond your ownership, you can rent them for around $500 per week."

Linking Statement

Earlier you were telling me…(link their most important emotional trigger before entering the suite.) Once you enter the suite, ask a Commitment Trial Closing question tying it back to their emotions.

Power Statement #5 (On the balcony in the model)

Please have room awareness when closing. You must not interfere with another broker's presentation.

Make a sweeping gesture with your arms and ask them excitedly, "What do you see?!" Wait for a response and they will typically say, "Skiers." "Ski Lift." "Mountains." "Blue sky" (usually *features*). "Tell me more!" They, or *you*, must switch to *advantages and benefits* and say, "Families having fun!" Let your clients share the joys of their observations. Compliment them on their experiences and choices and allow them to soak it all in! Once they are finished and there is silence, intensify your voice, and say, "Bob, what I see for you is that vacation to Hawaii! What I see is Maui. Kauai. Fiji. Bali! Mary, what I see for you is that vacation to Europe! What I see is Paris. Italy. Spain. Portugal! Grand Lodge on Peak 7, *this* premier ski in/ski out resort *will* get you there!!! With your permission, can I welcome you aboard as my newest owners!?" Assume the sale and extend your hand, "Bob and Mary, welcome aboard!"

If there is any hesitation or a "no," which means "not yet," keep the flow going. You must exclaim, "It doesn't get any better than this," and wait for a response. Your purpose is to flush out the true objection. "You told me earlier…", "Level with me…" and continue to sell and close by solving their problems or challenges.

"Think it and Link it."

~ Arda Linkin

Chapter 38

12. CLOSE

"MASTER CLOSERS accept full responsibility for their actions regardless of the outcome."

<u>CLOSE</u> –Welcome Your Newest Owners!

Closing techniques are not just the final step. That is why Trial Closes before the final CLOSE are so important. Always Trial Close and test the water before the final CLOSE. You should be trial closing and closing right after the INTENT TO SELL. Being a closer, you should already have used Compliance Trial Closes and Commitment Trial Closes throughout your presentation; starting with Compliance Trial Closing and moving toward Commitment Trial Closing. If you forgot the difference between the two types of closes, please go back and review. Study and master Compliance and Commitment Trial Closes. It is an essential piece of the puzzle, and they are the most important techniques of the sales process. You must be able to seamlessly transition and switch in a moment's notice between Compliance and Commitment Trial Closes. A good rule of thumb is when your client is becoming resistive because you are using Commitment Trial Closes, simply switch back into Compliance Trial Closes.

With practice you will develop unconscious competence to transition between Compliance and Commitment Trial Closes seamlessly and effortlessly. You will know when to move forward or back off a bit based on your clients' reactions and responses to your questions. You must observe your clients' body language to understand when you're being too aggressive. This is where you switch from Commitment Trial Closes (*pushing* too hard) back to Compliance Trial Closes (*pulling* your clients back in).

"You can't push a rope."

~ James "J.R." Roberts

Standing in the model is the most ideal time to close if it's the last part of your presentation. While in the model, ask, "What questions can I answer for you?" "Does the two bedroom look like it will work for you today?"

Back at the office, your clients may ask, "If we were to purchase today, what is the worst thing that could happen to us? Level with me, what is the downside of owning at this resort?" Your standard response, every time, should be, "In my most sincere opinion, the biggest downside is if you buy this today and then you don't use it. That is the biggest negative." At this time, you must keep quiet. Be silent, because, "He who speaks first loses." Your clients will always respond, "If we purchase here today, we would definitely use it. That would not be an issue." If your clients are on their way to becoming your newest owners, this is a perfect Baby Negative. Baby Negatives are extremely important. Baby Negatives are used to combat the objections: "This sounds too good to be true" or "This is too complicated" or "What other exaggerations, misinformation have you told me?".

Since your clients are asking new owner questions, at this moment, time is of the essence. So strike while the iron is hot! In your most enthusiastic voice and biggest smile extend your hand and say, "Welcome aboard!"

A manager can also be used at this time to reinforce what you have already said during our presentation. Managers provide a strong trust factor with regard to your efforts to close your clients, and frequently do a solid button up while moving forward to a sale. Remember, always be quiet and never speak once you have turned over your clients to your manager.

T.O. *Turn Over* your clients to a manager at your desk

Closing tools on the table for your manager:

- Worksheet-Filled out completely
- Rent Vs. Own Sheet
- Club Certificate
- Survey Sheet
- Exchange Directory

Once you *turn over* your clients to your Manager, *do not talk*! Silence is golden and your silence is essential!

"Bob and Mary, you remember, Dave. Dave, Bob and Mary would like to take their kids snowboarding, take advantage of the slope side parking and amenities pretty often, so the Club Membership is important to them. They would also use Getaways for occasional extra vacations. They would probably use their week here every few years, but mainly trade it to warm, sunny places. They would most likely use the Bonus Week from the Club Member Certificate for a second vacation somewhere here in Colorado."

"Owning with the Club Membership at a ski in/ski out resort would enable them to spend more time together away from their work and home, and according to Mary, have a closer relationship with their children. Bob and Mary came to the realization that their relationship with their family is what matters most, and this ownership program will force them to take vacations. Could you please help them with ownership? I have recommended a Summer Two Bedroom Annual ownership to them. They are happy with our program, but the money is just a little more than they are comfortable spending today. Earlier, you mentioned to me that we may have an owner who recently upgraded. Is that inventory still available?"

Again, keep quiet and let your manager build excitement and value, and look for buying signals. Every time you interrupt, you are pushing your client away from a sale. If your manager needs your advice, you will be asked for it directly.

"When a salesperson speaks *over* a T.O. manager
the deal is *over*."

~ Lost Wages

Sales Rules

Rule #1

Anything other than a "Yes" is a "No" (No means "Not Yet")

- How does this apply during your presentation?

- How can you prevent your clients from becoming evasive?

- During past presentations, have you "missed" or "bypassed" a sale because of a violation of Rule #1?

Rule #2

TODAY means "Initial Visit" (Continuous Tour Sequence)

- Why do you offer Initial Visit Incentives or First Day Incentives?

- Who takes advantage of these incentives?

- What prevents people from proceeding to take an action step here today?

- Where do you lose people in the presentation from taking an action step?

- How can you become better at your sales profession?

- When do you believe is the best time for clients to purchase your timeshare. Why? Elaborate on the subject of "Who benefits the most."

The middle class, average Joe: "All I want to purchase today is a four bedroom Christmas and New Year's Ownership."

~ Someday

Rule #3

It's Not Over Until It's Over!

- Explain what the above statement *truly* means to you.

- What traits do all Master Closers have in common?

- Explain why a Master Closer must have this essential mindset to close a sale.

- Why must your sales career be all consuming?

- What are you willing to give up in your personal life to be the best in your professional life?

Eight Goals of the Close

1. Save a valuable piece of information.

- What can you save?

- Why is that important?

- Once this valuable piece of information has been shared and your clients' emotional state has changed, continue to ask for the sale.

2. Slow down your speech, almost whisper and mirror your clients. Be like your clients because people like people just like themselves.

- What is the purpose of this method?

- Why is this an effective closing tool?

3. Everyone purchases everything on emotion as well as logic.

- Why is it important to close on emotion?

- Why is it important to close on logic?

- How do Master Closers "tie down" and get "buy in" on both emotion and logic?

- Please define "Master Closer." Are you a Master Closer? Why or why not?

4. Once you begin closing, attempt to get the deal before leaving your clients alone.

- Why do some Master Closers never leave their clients alone?

- Why do some Master Closers leave their clients alone?

- Which style do you prefer most of the time and why?

5. When closing and asking tough questions, he who speaks first loses.

- What is a tough question?

- Why must you ask tough questions?

- Do you agree that "He who speaks first loses" is an accurate statement? Why or why not?

6. When you don't get a "Yes," you must change the offer and add more value. Increase your enthusiasm!

- Please elaborate on any details regarding changing the offer, and explain why they are special.

- Why do you want to close a deal when the emotional state is high and positive?

- What value can you add?

7. Do not give up! Winners persist. Losers do not exist!

- Why do salespeople usually give up first?

- What does the word tenacity mean to you?

- What do the sayings "I was so close to a sale" and "I almost got the sale" mean to you?

- "You either get an A or an F in selling and closing." Please explain.

8. Always ask for the sale. In your sales presentation ask for the order today and earn their business.

- How do you ask for the order, sale and money? Please elaborate.

- Is closing the sale easy? Is it fun? Is it enjoyable?

- What does the statement "Closing is like having a sixth sense" mean to you?

- How can you become more competitive and tenacious?

When your clients are not being "real" with you:

- Not answering your questions directly
- Saying "Maybe" instead of "Yes" or "No"
- Giving false messages about what's important. For example, "I don't care about nice things," or, "I don't care about money."
- Misleading body language (the body never lies).

Deal with evasive clients and become a human lie-detector. You must address their evasiveness with an emotional statement such as, "Your kids want more of your time, not your money!"

You must get the mental attitude that you're not going to accept evasiveness from your clients. You're not going to take the no's. Start getting little yeses that will lead to the final yes. With every presentation you must do one of two things. You either;

1. Continue to sell and support your manager: If your manager is not getting the deal, and your clients pull you back into the conversation to repeat all the excuses why they are not going to buy, you must support your manager. Repeat and recap all of the benefits your clients shared with you, and Trial Close again. Ignore disparaging remarks, and continue to sell and close. It is time to get tough and mentally armed with knowledge so that you can anticipate and overcome consumer hesitations toward improving their lives.

2. Learn the real objection: You should never let your clients leave giving you false and misleading objections. It is your responsibility and duty to find out why they are saying "No." You must find the real reason that they are not buying so that you can learn from your mistakes and get better. This method is known as the "Lost Sale Close." Sometimes you can use it to continue to close, and then ask for the order again. Otherwise, the sale is truly lost. You can learn and earn respect from your clients by truly caring and asking them in a sincere way, "Where and when did I miss you?"

"Listen and learn from the best in your life.
Avoid the energy-takers that steal your power.
Your new inner circle will bring you freedom and joy."

~ Nakata

"More times than not, you will be rejected. You must work through rejection graciously and *learn something* from every presentation. Walk away to sell and close another day."

~ Warrior Spirit

Chapter 39

DYNAMIC PERSUASIVE VERBIAGES

"*MASTER CLOSERS* fearlessly improve their craft."

DYNAMIC PERSUASIVE VERBIAGES

Astonishing. Simple. Stupendous. Amazing. Fantastic. Impressive. Wonderful. Discover. Superb. Easy. Joyful. Guarantee. Health. Grateful. Happy.

Love. Money. New. Proven Results. Security. Safety. Save. Romance. You. Quality. Freedom. Adventure.

Use your clients' first names as often as possible. Clients love to hear their names.

The sales process is a transference of emotion. In order to get this to happen, you must ask involvement questions, and the magic will begin.

1. Are you starting to see the flexibility?

2. Are you starting to see the variety?

3. Isn't this different than what you thought it was going to be?

4. Can you see why so many families just like you are getting involved with us today?

5. Wouldn't you look toward your next vacation with greater anticipation if you knew you were going to stay with us?

6. Surely, you can see why so many people are jumping on this ground floor opportunity.

7. Isn't this different?

8. Isn't this better?

9. Clearly, you can see why our families are so excited to use their vacation homes.

10. Isn't living well life's best purpose?

11. You deserve this, and your family deserves this.

12. Isn't this what you work for?

13. Don't you deserve the best vacations possible?

14. Are you starting to see why so many owners join on their initial visit?

15. Are you starting to see why so many families choose vacation ownership with us?

16. We are getting better and better and better, don't you agree?

17. You must agree that we are better than the alternative!

18. Wouldn't you look forward to picking up the phone and going on vacation?

19. Wouldn't you be more productive at work if you knew a high quality vacation is waiting?

20. Have you ever realized a dream?

21. Do you want your children to realize their dreams?

22. If you have the wherewithal to come aboard here today, do you honestly feel that you and your children can dream together?

23. Remember, dreams can truly happen if, and only if, people have the courage to take an action.

24. Like, Use, Better Trial Closes:

Ask your clients; "Do you *Like* what you see?"

"If you were to purchase here today, would you *Use* it?"

"Wouldn't ownership be *Better* than the alternative?"

"Your newest owners are not trailblazers. Everyone is Doing It!"

~ B. Expectant

"React or Re-Act. Everyone deserves a second chance."

~ Fair Life

"Get busy living or get busy dying."

~ Shawshank

"Would've, Should've, Could've."

~ Man on his Dying Bed

Chapter 40

SELF EVALUATION

"MASTER CLOSERS: Be critical. Be very critical."

<u>SELF-EVALUATION</u>

1. Was my personal appearance appropriate?

2. Did I remember that my first impression to my clients was formed within the first 60 seconds?

3. Did I greet my clients immediately, or within the first two minutes?

4. Did I maintain the same feeling and attitude associated with my last sale before the greeting?

1) MEET and GREET (3-5 minutes)

1. "Hello, welcome to our resort, thank you for coming. Please call me (first name)"… remembering to smile and make eye contact!

2. Did I pay a sincere compliment?

3. Did I sincerely thank my clients for their valuable time and the opportunity to present to them?

4. Did I find any common ground?

5. Did I begin with easy, non-threatening questions?

6. Did I warm up my clients and establish credibility?

7. Did I establish like and trust by displaying "Kind Eyes"?

8. Did I offer a beverage before the WALL TOUR?

2) WALL TOUR (7-10 minutes)

1. Did I take control by leading my clients to the map, model and site plan?

2. Did I establish real estate value and scarcity of land at the map?

3. Did I show ARDA Awards and explain that with our proven performance we established our own reservation line?

4. Did I establish the credibility of my developer?

5. Did I introduce Phase selling?

6. Did I establish credibility of myself?

3) CLIENT PROFILE (12-15 minutes)

Basic 1   Front-End Bump (end of CLIENT PROFILE)

1. Did I take control of the seating arrangements?

2. Did I ask permission to ask questions?

3. Did I know all my CLIENT PROFILE questions in advance, and their purpose?

4. Did I ask opinion and feeling questions so that my clients could talk and reveal their needs?

5. Did I expand on questions and probe to get my clients to reveal and even more about themselves?

6. Did I demonstrate interest in my clients, and show them that I care?

7. Did I exercise the difficult discipline of listening? (How trust is born.)

8. What problems did I create?

9. Did my clients have a need or a vacation problem?

10. Did I have to create the needs or problems?

11. Did I discover whether or not my clients' vacation needs will be changing in the future?

12. Was relationship tension reduced (establishing friendship and trust)?

13. Did I acknowledge and speak equally to the husband and wife or significant others?

14. Did I ask questions and get commitments from the husband and wife or significant others?

15. Did I avoid interrupting my clients, or anxiously changing the subject?

16. Did I identify an emotional motivator such as adventure or quality time with family?

17. Did I like my clients?

18. Did my clients like me?

19. What was my clients' social style? Husband? Wife?

20. Did I demonstrate versatility by adjusting my social style temporarily to that of my clients?

21. Did I bring over a manager and introduce him as "my friend?"

22. Did I refrain from selling or giving my clients my recommendations too early in my presentation?

23. Did I focus on gathering information to use later?

4) RECAP (3 minutes)

1. Did I gain commitment from my clients that I got the RECAP right and that no matter what, they will continue to vacation?

2. Did I ask my clients if they had anything to add to my summary?

3. Did I feel the sale was made right here?

5) INTENT TO SELL (1 minute)

1. Did I show empathy?

2. Did I cover the agenda – what to expect, timing and tour sequence?

3. Did I deliver a convincing take away statement?

4. Did I properly introduce the First Day Incentives to purchase?

5. Did I build urgency through pricing and inventory?

6. Did I start Compliance Trial Closing, and then later use Commitment Trial Closing techniques?

6) WHY TODAY/CLUB CERT (5 minutes)

1. Did I blame the developer…no big deal?

2. Did I Trial Close and gain compliance with use and need?

3. Did I sell *features, advantages and benefits* addressing my clients' motives?

4. Did I internally remember the "Law of the Sale?"

5. Did I tie emotional motivators into the Club Certificate benefits?

6. Did I continuously tie in the Club Certificate through steps 6-12?

7. Did I break the pact *numerous* times through steps 6-12?

7) WHY VACATION (cover throughout)

1. Did I create any life problems, and then solve them through vacations?

2. Did I uncover any problems, and show my clients that vacations solve those problems?

8) EXCHANGE (10 minutes)

1. Did I Sizzle the exchange?

2. Did I sell in color using all five senses?

3. Did I use colorful language and lots of dynamic adjectives?

4. Did I put my clients in THEIR picture?

5. Did I strengthen or create a vacation commitment?

6. Did I keep it simple?

9) WHY TIMESHARE / RENT VS. OWN (7 minutes)

Basic 2   Conference (Prior to PRODUCT) (2 minutes)

1. Did I show my clients their vacation expenses in terms of time and money?

2. Did I talk about inflation?

3. Did I create value in deeded ownership?

4. Do they know their "Bundle of Rights" (Ownership, Exclusivity, Ability to Rent, Gift, Pass on in Estate?)

5. Did my upfront pricing make sense to my clients?

6. Did I show the 14.9% interest rate?

7. Did I show the 100% interest rate paid by renters which is 100% loss?

8. Did I tell Third-Party Stories (not about me, stories about my owners)?

9. Did my clients understand and believe that when they purchase their vacation accommodations that they are spending "anyway" money?

10. Did I ask my clients how long they were willing to collect hotel receipts?

11. Did I give my clients a task while I stepped away for a manager conference?

10) PRODUCT (8 minutes)

Basic 3   Worksheet (End of PRODUCT) (1 minute)

1. Did I customize my clients' use; pausing and Trial Closing after each segment of the product explanation?

2. Did I build and support strong value and interest in the Club Membership?

3. Did I build and support a strong value in ownership?

4. Did I present to my clients' specific needs, rather than tell all?

5. Did I use descriptive colorful words to put my clients in the picture?

6. Did I tell good third party stories using the technique of FEEL, FELT, FOUND?

7. How many third party stories did I use incorporating the five senses ?

8. How many features did I link to benefits to cause my clients to think, "What's In It For Me?" (WIIFM) What *features, advantages and benefits* did I show?

9. Did I create urgency and a strong need to own?

10. What was my clients' primary interest in ownership at our resort?

11. Did I completely fill out a worksheet 100 percent (no laziness)?

12. Did I isolate the down and monthly payment? Did I ask if the program was affordable TODAY? If it was not affordable, did I CHANGE THE DEAL?

11) PROPERTY/MODEL TOUR (time varies)

1. Did I use power statements at specific locations at the resort?

2. Did I ask enough Commitment Trial Closing questions?

3. Did I link specific amenities and services to my clients' emotional motivators (emotional reasons that my clients should purchase TODAY)?

12) CLOSE (however long it takes)

Basic 4   *T.O. Management Closing Assistance*

(Turn over the table with a positive and exciting RECAP)

1. How many buying signals did I get?

2. How many Commitment Trial Closes did I use?

3. Did I isolate to a single objection and bring a manager over to answer the objection to my clients' satisfaction?

4. How many times did I ask my clients to join?

5. Did I go the distance?

6. Did the tour result in a sale?

7. If no sale, why not?

8. What did I learn and what will I apply next time, next presentation, next client?

9. Did I use the technique "No Means Not Yet"?

10. Did I keep quiet after my manager took over the table?

11. Did I keep the end result in mind which is closing and getting a sale?

"When you close, you must have mental toughness and always go the extra mile. You must exude confidence, and always give sincere and extreme effort!"

~ Tenacious

Highlight the Activities in Your Resort Town!

Love your town! There are several reasons your resort was built where it is – the beauty of the area, the activities, the history, the fun, the food, the culture. Whatever it is that brings people into your town and keeps them coming back, write it out! When you compile a list of what makes your town special and present it to your clients, especially first time visitors, you'll be giving them a list of many things they will want to return for. Breaking it out by seasons will give winter visitors a peek at why summers are so popular, and Springtime visitors a glimpse of why they should return in the Fall. The more your clients see themselves visiting your town, the more attractive ownership at your resort will become.

We've put together a list of the seasonal activities and fun facts about Breckenridge, Colorado that you and your clients will explore and enjoy!

Why Breckenridge: Summer and Spring/Fall

- Best white water rafting in the country within an hour's drive
- ATV Tours
- Dirt Biking
- Gold Mine Tours
- Blue Ribbon Fly Fishing
- Hot Air Balloon flights
- Paintball
- Horseback Riding
- 200 miles of paved bike path around Summit County
- Throw your mountain bike on a chairlift (Never pedal uphill)

- Alpine Slide

- Miniature Golf

- Zip line

- 27 hole Jack Nicklaus designed golf course

- Camp Woodward (Practice flips for the winter in foam pits)

- Fishing on Lake Dillon

- Pontoon/Ski boat/Kayak the highest marina in the country

- Summit Hiking Guide (57 mountains in Colorado over 14,000 ft)

- Photograph wildlife

- Indoor Ice Skating Rink

- Hundreds of miles of mountain biking single track

- Fourth of July Parade and fireworks

- Dodge Viper Parade and Corvette week

- Beer, Music and Film Festivals, Wine Tastings, Oktoberfest

- Largest gold nugget found in the country (Tom's Baby, 14lbs)

- Summer Concert Series (National Repertory Orchestra) every week

- Farmer's Market

- Rubber Duck Race

- BBQ Competitions and BBQ on the beach (Spring Skiing)

- Ski until June (A-Basin)

- New year-round Alpine Coaster

Why Breckenridge: Winter

- Only town to ski into for Happy Hour

- 25,000 skiable acres within a 40 minute drive

- Highest chairlift in North America

- Two Nordic Centers

- Free cross country and snowshoeing at every trail head

- Snowmobiling

- Dog Sledding

- Dinner Sleigh Rides

- Sledding

- Outdoor Ice Skating or Indoor Ice Skating Rink

- 100 restaurants and bars on a mile long main street

- Oldest bar west of the Mississippi open through prohibition (Gold Pan)

- Hot Air Ballooning

- Horseback Riding

- Gondola Rides

- Ullr Fest (tribute to the Nordic god of winter)

- International Snow Sculptures

- Tubing hills with Magic Carpets

High Season and Slow Season Clients

Typically, high season WINTER travelers in Breckenridge have a vacation commitment because they have been skiing and snowboarding for years with their family anyway. High season SUMMER travelers usually enjoy mountain towns for the activities, cooler temperatures with less humidity and are frequently kid-centric. The slow season SPRING/FALL travelers tend to enjoy quieter times and by and large are budget-conscious. Slow season travelers might not be spending money for vacations and therefore they don't think they have a vacation commitment. They visit family, go camping or simply do not go on vacation (no vacation commitment). The emotional motivators (the emotional reasons that they will buy today) are different for clients visiting in each of the four seasons. You must be aware of which emotional motivators to discuss and *how* to discuss them. You must understand which emotional motivators not to discuss so that you don't *turn off* your clients. At times, what you don't say is more important than what you do say! You must possess the *wherewithal* to *read* your very *different season* clients.

Emotional Motivators (link these to your Club Certificate: First Day Incentives)

- Focus on friends and family reunions back at your resort for **PRESTIGE**

- Reframe time for retirement and make **DREAM** trips a reality

- Shorter trips to the mountains for **ROMANCE**

- Camp locally then Day Use for **SMART/FRUGAL** owners

- Gift Getaway trips to kids/family for history and **EDUCATION**

- Local road trips on the Travel Tab in Interval International for **ADVENTURE**

- Spring is less crowded, and quiet for **RELAXATION**

- Refer to kids/grandkids more for **NEW EXPERIENCES AND LEGACY**

- Second Home in the mountains for the whole family to **RECONNECT**

The Fundamentals of the Game

Pre-Game: Goal Setting

Physical Attitude

Mental Attitude

Focus

Preparation

Have a Personal Story

Practice

Product Belief

Hunger

Always Get Better

Intrinsic Traits: Professionalism

Enthusiasm

Patience

Confidence

Having Fun

Be a Team Player

In the Game: Eye Contact

Use Your Clients' Names

Smile

Listen

Find Common Ground

Entertain Your Clients

Get Your Clients Out of Their Comfort Zone

Take Control

Make Your Clients Ask Questions

Handle Objections

Ask Better Questions

Create / Find Problem(s)

Credibility

Use First-Party Stories

Use Third-Party Stories

Create a Higher Authority

Use Bumps

Build Value

Build Urgency

Use Analogies

Use Take Away Statements

Use Baby Negatives

Use Tie-Downs

Get Commitments

Be Consistent

Once the Sale Made, Stop Selling

"Vacation Ownership is all about helping people live well."

"Everyone leaves happy, regardless of the outcome!"

"May all your days be amazing. You only have one day at a time."

"There are no coincidences … more will be revealed."

~ McEneryism

Love where you live and work. Commitment to community, your company's culture and your ability to perform are paramount. Your main purpose is to make your Developer money. By doing so, you will make money. Money flows where energy goes. All is well, everyone is happy, all said and done.

May this book give you peace of mind, body and spirit. Face any uncertainty, difficulty, or adversity without fear. Find true passion within your "heart of hearts." Discover what you love most about your life and proceed with conviction.

Wisdom is a deep understanding and realization of people, things, events or situations resulting in the ability to choose, act or inspire to consistently produce optimum results with a minimum of time, energy or thought. It is the ability to optimally (effectively and efficiently) apply perceptions and knowledge to produce the desired results. Wisdom is also the comprehension of what is true or right coupled with optimum judgment as to action, discernment or insight. Wisdom often requires control of one's emotional reactions (the "passions") so that one's principles, reason and knowledge prevail to determine one's actions.

Courage (also bravery, fortitude, or intrepidity) is the ability to confront fear, pain, danger, uncertainty or intimidation. "Physical courage" is courage in the face of physical pain, hardship, death, or threat of death while "moral courage" is the ability to act rightly in the face of popular opposition, shame, scandal or discouragement.

I wish you the **Wisdom** and the **Courage** to apply all the techniques and principles in this book. Live and learn so that all your dreams come true with <u>IMMEDIATE SPEED</u>. Remember, it's no big deal, it's only timeshare … most of all, have fun and
Love Life!

Sincerely,

David McEnery

7964050R00160

Made in the USA
San Bernardino, CA
29 January 2014